D0323546

Jesus and Mary

In Praise of Their Glorious Names

by
Father Benedict J. Groeschel, C.F.R.

Our Sunday Visitor Publishing Division
Our Sunday Visitor, Inc.
Huntington, IN 46750

17 16 15 14 13 12   1 2 3 4 5 6 7 8 9

ISBN: 978-1-61278-624-7 (Inventory No. T1321)

eISBN: 978-1-61278-265-2

LCCN: 2012944349

Cover design: Lindsey Riesen

Cover art: The Crosiers

PRINTED IN THE UNITED STATES OF AMERICA

Dedication:

To two of New York's dedicated archbishops:
Edward Cardinal Egan
Timothy Cardinal Dolan
and to the memory of a third,
John Cardinal O'Connor

Acknowledgments

One rainy day in October, my good friend Bert Ghezzi of Our Sunday Visitor came from his home in Florida to visit me in New York. He brought with him the idea for this book, which he thought would be a good project for me. I must confess that I was a little resistant at first. I was beginning to think my writing days had come to an end, and (especially on a bleak and rainy day) I didn't feel like committing myself to something new. But Bert is wonderfully persuasive, and in short order he managed to make me very enthusiastic about this project. I thank him for that; this book has been a pleasure to write, and a very prayerful part of my days for several months now. I hope he is pleased with the result.

I would like to thank John Collins, my editor, for all his help.

I also thank a priest friend of mine who was of great assistance in the writing of this book.

CONTENTS

Introduction

I want to make one thing perfectly clear from the outset: This is a devotional book and certainly not a theological one. I am very pleased to report that there are still decent numbers of Catholics and other Christians whose spiritual lives center on devotion in various forms. They believe very strongly that devotion has deepened and strengthened their relationship with God, with Our Lady, and with the saints. They assert that devotion lends intensity and a joyful vibrancy to their prayer lives. I admit — a little proudly — that I am among those people. From the earliest days of my childhood, I was immersed in a Catholic culture that was intensely devotional. In those days devotion seemed to be in the very air we breathed. It permeated every aspect of our lives. Christ, Our Lady, and the saints were not just real to us, but very present, and the devotions we pursued kept us constantly aware of this holy and loving presence in our day-to-day lives. Many objects related to devotional practices, such as statues and holy pictures, were common in our homes. Others, such as rosaries, were always in our pockets, and we used them to pray as we walked. Still others, like the Miraculous Medal, hung around our necks every day, the image of Our Lady constantly close to our hearts.

Devotion and devotions, however, fell on rather hard times after the Second Vatican Council. Imbibing perhaps too much of the surrounding culture's excessive rationalism and skepticism, we began to feel a bit ashamed of our devotional practices. After nourishing us for centuries, these practices suddenly seemed old-fashioned and perhaps even Old World. The regular Monday evening devotions to Our Lady of the Miraculous Medal, which formerly had filled whole churches throughout the country, became sparsely attended. Novenas were forgotten. Dramatic images were removed from our churches and replaced with cool, almost abstract representations of Christ and the saints. Tragically, even the Holy Rosary was thought, in some Catholic circles, to be old-fashioned and not worth the effort.

The idea behind all this, I imagine, was that we were supposed to have progressed beyond the need for such aids and gateways into prayer. I believe it was also because certain types of emotions — the kinds that may at times appear to be sentimental — came to be looked down upon. They were considered childish, inauthentic, perhaps stumbling blocks rather than aids to prayer. The unstated idea was that a mature relationship with God was built on an intellectual foundation. We have seen the same ideas affect the celebration of the Mass. Someone once told me that he thought many priests celebrated the *Novus Ordo* as if it were a Mass for saints, for those who have no need of any external aid but who can simply plunge into a close relationship with Christ and a profound awareness of the reality of the Eucharist with no preparation. Ordinary people (You know who they are — You and I!) have trouble putting their day-to-day lives behind them without the many aids that were once so generously supplied by the Church: the hushed surroundings, so separate from the outside world; the sight and scent of incense slowly wafting upward, as if to heaven; the measured, deliberate, and carefully choreographed gestures of the celebrant; the sound of Gregorian chant, so ethereal that it seemed to be the song of angels. We flesh-and-blood creatures often need such things during Mass to remind us that, for the moment at least, we have separated ourselves from the ordinary world to enter an extraordinary one, a world in which we are in the presence of something special, something unutterably sacred. Without the help of these externals, the very presence of Christ among us can sometimes go unnoticed.

Devotion has been defined in many ways. I think the simplest definition, however, is to say that it is a way of entering into prayer that gives as much emphasis to the heart as it does the mind. Devotion answers the deep needs of our souls. It implies a trust in the emotions, as well as a willingness to use those emotions to deepen our encounters with God in prayer. When we use the term "devotion" in this way we are saying that we approach God, Our Lady, and the saints not simply with serene thoughts or elegant prayers, but with sighs and groans and perhaps even tears. Devotion is at home with images, and many of the titles of Our Lady and our Divine Savior that are discussed in this book have icons, pictures, or statues intimately associated with them. In many cases, the image came first and the devotion grew later. Who doesn't know what the image of the Sacred Heart looks like? Who doesn't know Our Lady of Perpetual Help? These are devotional images.

Devotion allows us to approach God with our imagination. Now, this is not to say that in devotional prayer we make things up.

And I am emphatically not saying that God or the saints or Our Lady are products of our imaginations. I am simply saying that devotion shows us that imagination can be a vital and creative part of our spiritual lives. Here are words concerning devotion that were written by a secular anthropologist whose field is the study of religious faith in its various forms. They could have been written by any devout Catholic:

> [T]o know God intimately, you need to use your imagination, because the imagination is the means humans must use to know the immaterial. This, by the way, is something the church fathers knew well. For Augustine, the road to God ran through the mind. It is our own peculiar era that equates the imagination with the frivolous and the unreal. That is why contemporary Christians sometimes get nervous about the word *imagination*.[1]

Our faith needs a strong devotional dimension because when we are truly grasped by faith, it is not simply the rational part of us that is grasped: we are grasped as a totality. Our hearts and minds and souls are different facets of our one being. They must work in harmony if they are to work at all as we respond to God's love and graces. To respond to God authentically is to respond as a whole person. A purely intellectual response to faith is inadequate, and perhaps bloodless. If the mind does not work in concert with the heart, faith will become dry, something small that can be tucked away in one corner of the mind. Eventually, it will probably wither away. That is why I have always encouraged devotion and continue to do so.

In this little book, we will be looking in a truly devout way at some of the many titles that have been given throughout the Christian centuries to our Blessed Mother and to our Lord Jesus Christ. Some of these titles, like the "Good Shepherd," have been culled from holy Scripture; others, such as "Mary, Help of Christians," have developed in various places and at various times in the Church's history, often in response to the needs of a specific time. Still others, such as "Healer of Shattered Hearts" are more modern, but are very consistent with the way the Church has thought during its many centuries.

All these titles arose out of the efforts of devout people to express some particular aspect of their understanding of our Divine

1 Tanya Luhrmann, "Why Woman Hear God More than Men Do," *Christianity Today*, May 2012 (Web only).

Savior or His Blessed Mother, some quality that may be difficult to express in words but which speaks to people in ways that are deeper than mere words. In this book, we will examine many titles, looking at them through the eyes of faith and with the aid of the wonderful imagination with which we have been blessed by God. We will try to find in each one something that touches us, something that tugs a bit at our hearts, something that lets us see things just a bit more clearly. We will use primarily, but not exclusively, two wonderful sources of titles of Our Lord and Our Lady: *The Litany of the Holy Name of Jesus* and *The Litany of Loreto*. Each of these litanies has been part of the prayer life of the Catholic Church for centuries, and each provides a wonderful source of titles and names upon which we can meditate. Most Catholics, especially those of my generation and older, will be familiar with these litanies and will remember praying them often in their youth.

As you can see, this is a short book, one that could easily be read in a few hours. However, I hope you will not read it that way. I hope you will read it carefully and with real devotion. I suggest that you read just one or perhaps two sections a day and that you read them slowly and prayerfully. I hope that in that way each section can become a source of prayer and meditation that will stay with you for that day, and perhaps beyond. As you delve ever deeper into the meanings behind the titles of Our Lord and Our Lady, I hope you will deepen your relationship with them and perhaps see their importance in your life in a clearer and more profound way.

The Significance of Names and Titles

When we read a litany, we are confronted with many names and many titles. I hope that this will make us aware of the significance of names in ways that we were not before. In our time and in our culture, we often overlook the importance of names, the value of titles, as we overlook so many things. Yet our biblical tradition reminds us that names and titles are of great importance. In the Ten Commandments we are told never to take the name of God in vain. In both ancient and contemporary Judaism we find a profound reverence for the name of God. In ancient Judaism, God's name was considered so holy that it was never to be uttered except by the high priest, and then only once every year as he entered the Holy of Holies in the Temple. Even today, the name of God is never voiced or even written by a devout Jew. He will always substitute a title like "*Adonai,*" which means "my lord," or sometimes he will simply say "*Hashem,*" which literally means "the name."

Christianity shows a similar reverence for the name of Jesus. Up until fairly recently, it was an almost universal custom for Catholics to bow their heads when they said or heard the name of our Divine Savior. Sadly, this custom has been nearly lost in recent years. It would be wonderful if it came back. If you went to Catholic schools when I did, the sisters saw to it that when the name of Jesus was uttered every head in the classroom bowed — immediately and practically in unison! In fact, we almost thought that if we failed to bow our heads we were straying close to sin.

Along with the sacred names come the titles. The most obvious of these — although one we may not always think about — is Jesus Christ. We have a tendency to say this name and title of our Divine Savior as if the two words were a first and last name. They certainly are not. The word "Christ" is a form of a Greek word that means "anointed." Thus, when we say "Jesus Christ" we are really saying "Jesus the anointed one" or "Jesus, Who is the Christ — the Messiah."

Our Lord and Our Lady are the two primary titles that we use in English; of course, they indicate the reverence that we should have toward their bearers. Much more elaborate titles such as "Savior of the World" have become an important part of Catholic piety. Many such titles are poetic and evocative and attempt to describe the indescribable. They open a window for us to view our Divine Savior or His mother, and have the capacity to teach or show us something. Again, in the rather vague and unpoetic times in which we live, these ideas are lost, especially by younger Catholics. It is my hope and prayer that in some small way thiAAAs book will help to remedy that problem.

Let us begin our meditation on the holy names of our Divine Savior and His Blessed Mother with a short poem that I read over and over again as I was preparing to write this book. I hope you will approach it slowly, carefully, and in a truly devout way. Let its images seep into your consciousness, for it says in a few shimmering words much of what I have tried to say in this entire book.

Mary the Dawn

Mary the dawn, Christ the Perfect Day;
Mary the gate, Christ the Heavenly Way!
Mary the root, Christ the Mystic Vine;
Mary the grape, Christ the Sacred Wine!
Mary the wheat, Christ the Living Bread;
Mary the stem, Christ the Rose blood-red!
Mary the font, Christ the Cleansing Flood;
Mary the cup, Christ the Saving Blood!
Mary the temple, Christ the temple's Lord;
Mary the shrine, Christ the God adored!
Mary the beacon, Christ the Haven's Rest;
Mary the mirror, Christ the Vision Blest!
Mary the mother, Christ the mother's Son
By all things blest while endless ages run. Amen.

— Anonymous

1
Mary, the Morning Star

"Rejoice, Mother of Light:
Jesus, the sun of justice,
overcoming the darkness of the tomb,
shed his radiance over the whole world."

— Entrance antiphon, Mass of the Virgin Mary
and the Resurrection of the Lord

Let us imagine for a moment that it is night, a night that has been very long and difficult. In fact, it has seemed endless. Peaceful oblivion — sleep's usual gift to us — is elusive. Despite our constant yearnings, slumber maddeningly remains beyond our grasp. A vague fear grips us. We struggle to identify it, but cannot, for it has no real source, no name. It is clear that anxiety and uncertainty will be our only companions until the dawn, and we feel very, very alone. Darkness is everywhere, wrapping itself around us like a heavy blanket. It is as if we are nothing.

Now let us imagine that this darkness, this awful night, is not a literal darkness but the metaphorical darkness of a world lost to sin. It is the darkness of a world that has become so estranged from God that it cannot even envision what forgiveness and reconciliation might be, what the love of God might be. This is the world as it was before the life, death, and resurrection of Jesus Christ came like a bright and blazing sun to scatter the darkness and replace it with a light that can never be dimmed.

We must never forget that this birth of light into our world comes only as the result of our Blessed Mother's holy acceptance of the will of God. "Let it be to me according to your word" (Lk 1:38), she says, and with these words Mary becomes the harbinger of light, the bearer of God's eternal light into a darkened and lost world.

The Church refers to this when she calls our Blessed Mother by the beautiful and poetic title of "Morning Star." A morning star is a star that seems larger and brighter than those of the night sky; the morning star rises over the horizon just before dawn, like a messenger. It seems to announce that the reign of night is about to come to an end, that the dawn will soon arrive. What a perfect symbol this is for

Our Lady, for she is so much like that star. The luster of her sinlessness and purity stand out against the darkness of the entire world, reminding us over and over again that the light of God is never far away and that it can never be overcome.

Darkness enters our lives in various ways. Some of us become lost to sin; some feel overcome by tragedy; some are simply deadened by disappointment. Sometimes, a dark and nameless emptiness closes in on us until we feel it has permeated our entire being. When we are faced with such darkness — and at some point we are all faced with it — we would do well to turn to our Blessed Mother. Light was born to the world through her. Light can be born to each individual life through her, as well. We must never lose sight of the fact that she is our Morning Star, shining brilliantly in even the darkest of nights. She is the messenger from God who comes with the glad tidings that night is never eternal; that the light of Christ is capable of illuminating the shadows through which we walk, of scattering the darkness of our lives, of obliterating even the gloom of death.

Prayer

Mother of Christ, Morning Star and bright dawn of the new creation, open our hearts to the pure light of grace that enters infallibly into the darkness of our world. As your immaculate soul signaled the definitive end to the power of evil in this world, so also shine your gracious light upon our sins and failings and turn us to the source of all Light, Jesus Christ, who is Lord forever and ever. Amen.

2

Jesus, King of the Universe

"Lord of the ages evermore,
Each nation's King, the wide world o'er,
O Christ, our only Judge thou art,
And Searcher of the mind and heart."

— From a hymn from First and Second Vespers
of the Solemnity of Christ the King

How often do you contemplate the vastness of the universe? I suspect it is very seldom. We are too wrapped up in ourselves and the things that affect us directly to give much attention to the overwhelming extent of God's creation, to the seeming endlessness of existence. For us, the universe is usually subjective, consisting of what we've experienced in our very limited lives. Perhaps astrophysicists are constantly aware that the universe is of unfathomable dimensions and impenetrable mystery. But the rest of us live as if only a little segment of our miniscule planet existed. Think about this fact, and also about a question it raises: Does our narrow vision of creation result in a narrowed understanding of the Source of that creation, of God, of Christ?

Go outside late some night and gaze at the sky. If you're lucky enough to live not too near the bright lights of a city, you will be able to get a sense of the immensity of creation. The stars will seem numberless. Some are so far away that their light will have taken years — sometimes even centuries — to get to earth. Yet all the stars you see are within our own galaxy, and there are thousands of galaxies, many of them much larger than ours. Such immensity staggers the mind. It also forces us to acknowledge something we like to ignore: our own comparative insignificance. "What is man that thou art mindful of him" (Ps 8:4) an ancient psalmist asks of God. Think of the psalmist's question as you gaze at the stars, and try to answer it honestly. For the agnostic or the atheist, as well as for followers of most of the religions that have existed on our little planet, the answer to this question is bleak: we are little or nothing, a passing shadow. But for the Christian, the question and its answer should fill us with joy: we are the ones so beloved of God that He gave His only begotten Son for us.

This startling contrast should fill us with awe, with endless wonder and thanksgiving. The immensity of God's love, infinitely surpassing even the immensity of the universe, is showered upon us — creatures who seem too insignificant even to be worthy of Divine notice! As you gaze at the night sky, remember that all you see exists through the Word of God who became incarnate for us as Jesus of Nazareth. The famous words of Saint John's Gospel teach us that "all things were made through him, and without him was not anything made that was made" (Jn 1:3). The vast expanse of the cosmos exists because of Jesus, who was born a helpless child in Bethlehem. Planets, stars, and galaxies silently wend their way through endless space at the bidding of Jesus, a carpenter in ancient Judea. All that is visible, as well as dimensions that we cannot perceive or imagine, bow to Jesus, who was put to death on a wooden cross. The Word of God rules over all things as King of the universe. Yet, the Word of God is Jesus of Nazareth who loves us so deeply that He becomes our spiritual food in the Eucharist.

Jesus is King of the Universe. As such, He is greater than any king who has existed or ever will exist. Kings are symbols of ultimate authority, but Jesus *is* ultimate authority. He is also the King who humbles himself, taking part in our seemingly insignificant lives and thus raising those lives to incomparable significance, making them worthy of eternity.

As you look at the stars, remember that they are not there by accident. Remember that they have a King, a King who is infinity — infinity who chose to become finite for us when we were lost and hopeless. This King of the Universe — Jesus Christ — has the authority to rule over all things with unimaginable power. Yet, He will not command us. He will humbly ask us to open our hearts and souls to Him. If we do, we can be sure that He will be a King who rules over us with unimaginable love.

Prayer

O glorious King of the Universe, Jesus Christ, to You we turn with confident hope that You will reconcile all things in heaven and on earth and lead our souls to salvation. Make us partners in Your saving work and help us to bring the whole world to experience the wonders of Your kingdom, who live and reign with the Father and the Holy Spirit, now and forever. Amen.

3

Mary, Ark of the Covenant

> "O noble Virgin, truly you are greater than any other greatness. For who is your equal in greatness, O dwelling place of God the Word? To whom among all creatures shall I compare you, O Virgin? You are greater than them all, O Ark of the Covenant, clothed with purity instead of gold! You are the ark in which is found the golden vessel containing the true manna, that is, the flesh in which divinity resides."
>
> — Saint Athanasius of Alexandria, from *The Homily of the Papyrus of Turin*

We are all familiar with the Old Testament story of Noah's ark. From our earliest childhood we were told of forty days and forty nights of rain, of the flood, and of the animals who survived to repopulate the world only because Noah had built a ship so large that it could hold two of every species. If any biblical tale seemed fit for Hollywood, it is surely that of Noah's ark. Yet there is another Old Testament narrative that involves an ark, and this is one that few Catholics seem to know very much about. In the Book of Exodus, we read of the Ark of the Covenant. This ark, however, is not a ship, but an ornate chest or box, one that the Children of Israel reverently carried with them throughout forty years of desert wanderings. Containing the tablets of the Law, the symbol of the covenant between God and the Children of Israel at Mount Sinai, this Ark was the most precious possession of the Israelites. It was valuable to them not because of what it was made of, or even because of what it contained, but because it assured the people of the Divine Presence (the *Shechina* in Hebrew, a word which comes from a root that means to dwell). Scripture tells us that this Divine Presence — and surely that must mean the Holy Spirit — hovered over the Ark of the Covenant like a cloud, filling the tent in which the Ark was kept. In other words, God literally dwelt with the people as long as the Ark was present. This very tangible presence of God was constant proof to the Israelites that their divine covenant remained in force, that God would never desert them, that they were still His chosen ones. Thus the Ark was not simply the center of ancient Israelite religious life, it was the center of their hope.

At Trinity Retreat, where I live, we have an especially beautiful icon of Our Lady. It depicts the Blessed Mother with her hands prayerfully uplifted the way a priest's hands often are during Mass.[2] This position subtly suggests Our Lady's complete openness to and acceptance of God's will. The Divine Infant is shown in a circular shape, which is in front of her, obscuring the middle part of her body. In the circle with the Infant are bright stars and the night sky, with light surrounding the darkness — the universe. As you look at the icon, you can't help but realize that the placement of the circle suggests that the Child and the universe are really within the figure of Mary, within her womb awaiting birth — awaiting the new creation. The following quotation from the Eastern Liturgy of Saint Basil expresses in words something very similar to the meaning of this icon: "In You, O Full of Grace, all creation rejoices, O Sanctified Temple, Mystical Paradise. He made your womb a throne, more spacious than the heavens."

This icon could be titled the Ark of the New Covenant, for Our Lady, like the Ark in the Book of Exodus, is nothing less than the dwelling place of God in our world. As the Ark bore the tablets that signified the Old Covenant, she — in her very body — bears the One whose blood would be "shed for many" in establishing a new and eternal covenant. As Mary gives her "yes" to God's plan, she allows the divine and the human to dwell together in a way the ancient Israelites in the Sinai desert could never have imagined; she allows the impossible to happen. She allows God to become man.

What more intimate relationship can there be than that between a mother and her child? What extravagant love is shown by the Source of all being as He permits himself to be held lovingly within the womb of a young woman. Here God comes to dwell not just among us as did the cloud of Divine Presence in the desert, but to enter directly into our fragile lives, to live our fears and experience our pains.

Mary is the Ark of the New Covenant, and this is something we must never forget. As such, she is the bearer of eternal hope into our world.

---

2 This is usually called the *orans* position.

Prayer

Holy Mary, Ark of the Covenant and first tabernacle of the Bread of Life, in you we find all the treasures of wisdom and holiness. Pour forth into our hearts the wealth of God's covenant love for mankind, and give us strength to persevere in our journey to reach the joys of heaven. We ask this through our Lord Jesus Christ, who lives and reigns forever and ever. Amen.

4
Jesus, Father of the World to Come

"For no other reason did Christ descend to earth
with its metal barriers that block eternity
but to crack those bronze doors and smash their iron bars
and thereby lead us away from corruption to himself
and make us free instead of slaves."

— Saint Anastasius of Antioch,
from a homily on the resurrection of Christ

When we contemplate a title such as Jesus, Father of the World to Come, we must be very aware that we have moved into the realm of the mysterious and the absolute. Yet, at the same time, we cannot help but realize that we have also arrived at the most basic yearning of the human heart, the yearning for continuance, for life that does not end in oblivion. As human beings created in the image of God, we are blessed with reason and understanding. With these gifts, however, comes awareness of our finitude, of death — of our inevitable end. The Old Testament expresses this in poignantly poetic terms: "Man that is born of woman is of few days and full of trouble. He comes forth like a flower and withers; he flees like a shadow, and continues not" (Jb 14:1-2). We do indeed seem to be like flowers or shadows, creatures that exist for a brief moment only to disappear forever. Many people strive for their whole lives to deny this truth, but it is too real to be denied forever. Each of us must one day confront the fact that there will come a time when we will be gone from our little planet, a time when even the last memory of us will be gone.

Such an awareness can easily lead to despair, to a sense of meaninglessness, and it has done so for countless people over the centuries. However, there should be no cause for despair in anyone who truly knows Jesus Christ. The life, death, and resurrection of Jesus Christ teach us something that obliterates despair. Christ teaches us that those famous words from the Song of Songs, attributed to Solomon, "Love is strong as death" (8:6), are not simply poetry. They are literal truth. They are the truth that saves us.

I would like you to ponder for a moment the infinite love of God for us. Imagine the love that caused God to send His only

Son to share our human life, to subject himself to all the uncertainties and anxieties, the fears and terrors and limitations that are part of the human condition, to give himself in agonizing death for us. What greater love can exist than this? It is this love, manifest in every moment of Jesus' earthly life, which is literally more powerful than death. This love reaches beyond the depths of our despair and our human finitude to grant us something to which we have no real right: the gift of eternity. It is because of this love that the finality of death is at last overthrown. Jesus shows us a love that is so great we can barely imagine it, a love that is so great it refuses to permit the human soul to cease to be. The love of God literally refuses to surrender us to nothingness.

"Love demands infinity,"[3] wrote Joseph Ratzinger years before he became Pope Benedict XVI. In these wise words we see what it really is to call Jesus "Father of the World to Come." He is the One who has gone before us into death and triumphed over it out of love for us. He is the One who offers us a world that cannot die, who offers us a relationship that cannot wither. He is the One who leads us from the tumult of earthly life into the peace of a life that cannot end, a life in which every sadness has become joy.

Prayer

O good Jesus, Father of the World to Come and lover of all You have created, please send Your most Holy Spirit to inspire us to set our hearts always in the world that never ends. Keep us free from sin in this life and make us strong witnesses to the joy that never ends. We ask this with confidence in Your infinite grace and mercy. Amen.

3 Cardinal Joseph Ratzinger, *Introduction to Christianity* (San Francisco: Ignatius Press, 1990), p. 230.

5
Mary, Mother of God

> "Though still a virgin she carried a child in her womb,
> and the handmaid and work of his wisdom
> became the Mother of God."
>
> — Saint Ephraim of Syria, from *Songs of Praise*

As Catholics, we refer to our Blessed Mother as the "Mother of God" all the time, and, what's more, we are inclined to do so rather casually. We address Our Lady under this title repeatedly whenever we pray the Rosary: "Holy Mary, Mother of God, pray for us sinners." More often than not we utter these words as if the expression "Mother of God" were the most natural thing in the world to say. But I would like you to stop for a moment and think about this title in a very prayerful way. Perhaps you might imagine that you have never heard it before. Say it over and over in your mind slowly and meditate on it — Mary, Mother of God. If we think about these words clearly for even a few moments, I am sure that most of us will realize that this is a title of profound mystery, of paradox. How can it be possible for a woman who came into being at a specific moment and in a specific place to be the mother of the eternal God? In other words, how can the finite give birth to the infinite? Here we find a title of Our Lady that expresses something that the rational mind tells us is impossible. Because of God's humility and overwhelming love for us, however, the impossible has become possible.

The Second Person of the Blessed Trinity became incarnate for us out of love. In profound humility the limitless God not only took on our flesh and blood but the limitations that attend every human life, including even the death that each of us must one day face. Christ possesses both a divine and a human nature, but these natures are perfectly united in the one person who was born of Mary in Bethlehem, preached in Judea, and eventually died on a cross. Can there be a greater act of divine humility than that of becoming so deeply joined to the one aspect of creation that struggles against and tries to reject God's love?

So when Mary gave birth to Jesus, she gave birth to all that Jesus was and is — not just His humanity, but also to His divinity. Although it is an absurdity to say that she gave birth to God in eternity, or that she gave birth to the Second Person of the Blessed Trinity, we can still say that she is truly the Mother of God, for Jesus truly is both God and man. She, who was finite, was the one who enabled God to enter our human finitude, to enter into and participate in our living and dying, to share our fragile hopes and our many terrors, and to offer us salvation.

"Virgin Mother of God, He whom the whole world cannot contain enclosed himself as a child within your womb," reads the Entrance Antiphon for the Feast of Mary the Mother of God. How overwhelmed with gratitude we should be when we read these words and when we contemplate the infinite love and humility that God demonstrates by choosing Mary of Nazareth to be His mother ... and in so doing, choosing us to be His brothers and sisters.

Prayer

Dearest Mary, whom we invoke as Mother of God and our own loving Mother, turn our hearts away from petty things and give us grace to be concerned only about the things of God, as you were in your earthly life. Accept and bless our efforts to bring all souls to Christ, who lives and reigns with the Father and the Holy Spirit, now and forever. Amen.

6
JESUS, AUTHOR OF LIFE

"What is urgently called for is a general mobilization of consciences
and a united ethical effort to activate a great campaign in support of life.
All together, we must build a new culture of life."

— Pope John Paul II, encyclical *Evangelium Vitae*, 1995

In chapter three of the Acts of the Apostles, we read of Saint Peter using a term that continues to have great relevance for us today. He notes the shocking fact that the people of his day called for the release of a murderer, Barabbas, in order to hand over to death "the Author of Life" (Acts 3:15), Jesus Christ. Think about this for a moment. Peter did not call Jesus the author of a book, a project, a great piece of music. He called Him the "Author of Life" itself. The life-versus-death contrast is striking in Saint Peter's words: One who destroys life is spared so that the very Author of Life can be destroyed. The starkness of this thought stops us in our tracks. Yet, it shouldn't, for this contrast is part of our daily lives, and we rarely notice it. Every day, we see death encroach on life. Think about how the things of the natural world decay and die. Notice the effects of illness and age in your own body. Look at all the sin and crime in the streets. The life-versus-death drama is woven into the very fabric of our fallen world. Of course, we should always be on the side of life, but I can't say that we humans always do very well in that particular fight. We need someone to help us overcome the forces of deterioration, decay, and death, which are not just all around us, but even within us. The only one equipped to show us the way is the One who conquered death and now lives forever.

Let me tell you, as someone who experienced a serious car accident several years ago, perhaps I have a better appreciation of the Author of Life than most do. People tell me — I don't remember it myself — that I was actually dead for twenty-seven minutes that night. The medical personnel had given up on me, but my good friend Father John Lynch would not give up; he continued to pray fervently and to beg the emergency medical technicians to continue their efforts, which they did, somewhat reluctantly. The unexpected happened, and afterward no one could explain my "resurrection" after being dead for so long. I was told by mystified doctors that there was no explanation. As a Catholic, I needed no medical explanation. I knew why I was still alive, and who brought me back from the edge of eternity. Jesus wanted me here on this earth a little longer. When the Author of Life gives you the incomparable gift of life, you can presume that there is a good reason for it — even if you can't figure out what it is.

God, in His mercy, taught me a very fundamental lesson from that earth-shattering event. He taught mem in the depths of my being, that human life, though fragile, is also sacred. I always knew the Church's teaching on the sanctity of life, of course, but because of my own brush with death, I now understood as never before that Jesus is the only one who has authority (from which we get the term author) over life and death. I think I am more dedicated than ever to help in the effort to win this victory over death with Him.

My great priest friend of many decades, Msgr. Philip Reilly of Brooklyn, N.Y., is the leader of a wonderful movement called Helpers of God's Precious Infants. I don't think that there is anyone in the world who has done more to save babies from abortion than this man.

The most extraordinary accomplishment of Msgr. Reilly has been his ability to get the Church, including many priests and bishops, out to abortion centers. He focuses his work on the Author of Life in the Eucharist, and on Mary in the Rosary. He celebrates Mass in a parish near an abortion center. After Mass, a few people remain praying in front of the exposed Blessed Sacrament while the rest of the people walk to the abortion mill while praying the Rosary. They finish with a moment of silent prayer for the abortion personnel and then return to the church for Benediction. It's really that simple, but innumerable conversions, last-minute changes of mind, and clinic closures have resulted from these efforts. The Author of Life is brought by the faithful to the places of death, accompanied by Mary and her Rosary.

Prayer

Lord of all and Author of Life, graciously let a ray of Your Life penetrate our darkened hearts and make us see the immense value of life around us. Allow us to be witnesses of the sanctity of life everywhere we go so that we may proclaim the victory of life in time and eternity. We ask this in Your most holy Name. Amen.

7

Mary, the Mother of Christ

"... and lo, the star which they had seen in the East went
before them,
till it came to rest over the place where the child was.
When they saw the star, they rejoiced exceedingly with
great joy;
and going into the house they saw the child with Mary his
mother,
and they fell down and worshiped him.
Then, opening their treasures, they offered him gifts,
gold and frankincense and myrrh."

— Matthew 2:9-11

Think about what an impact this scene must have had on Our Lady. What emotions must have been stirred up within her at the arrival of such strange guests, guests who dressed in a type of finery she had never seen and who came from faraway places that she could never visit. We are inclined to imagine Our Lady as she is depicted on the Miraculous Medal: as Queen of Heaven. We forget that at the time of Jesus' birth Mary was a simple Jewish peasant girl, a very young woman who seemed to differ little from a thousand other girls in Judea. Yet by the time these guests arrived, this young woman's life had already been transformed irrevocably, turned on its head in an unimaginable and possibly terrifying way. She was the new mother of a child who was different from all children who had ever been born and different from all children who would ever be born.

Can we imagine that she was not bewildered and even frightened? Can we imagine that she really grasped that the helpless newborn in her arms was the infinite God to whom she prayed? Perhaps she understood little in those early days; maybe she even dared to hope that her life would become normal, ordinary — safe — once more.

But any such hope would surely have been dispelled with the arrival of the Magi. Men of worldly wisdom, of wealth and power, were suddenly in her little home, falling to their knees and prostrating themselves before her and her son. Their treasure boxes revealed gifts the likes of which she had never known. Softly glimmering gold, the possession of a king, was laid at her feet. Sweet smelling frankincense, to be used at the altar of a god, was offered to her child. But when the third gift was revealed a shadow must have fallen across Mary's heart. It was myrrh, to be used in anointing the body of a loved one for burial. Perhaps Mary turned away at the sight of this third gift; surely, she must have clutched her son closer to herself, trying to protect Him from this startling reminder of what He and she must one day face.

No matter what Mary thought before the arrival of the Magi, she surely must have understood after it, that there was to be no normal life for her and her child. She must have clearly understood that her son had been chosen not simply for great things, but for the work of God, chosen to be both king and martyr. Was that the moment when she fully comprehended that the Messiah — the Christ — for whom her people longed, and for whom she had been taught to pray, was the child she held in her arms?

"You are the Christ, the Son of the living God" (Mt 16:16), confessed Saint Peter, and this is usually considered the first moment when the nature of Jesus as Messiah was known. Although it is certainly the first moment in holy Scripture, it is not the first moment in history, for Mary, who pondered so many things deep "in her heart" (see Lk 2:19) lived quietly with this reality for more than thirty years before Peter uttered his famous words. She lived as the Mother of Christ, the mother of the Anointed One who was to bring hope into a hopeless world. She watched with a mother's loving gaze as He grew older, knowing that every day brought Him closer to the time when He would leave her and begin His work, work that would lead to tragedy.

We call Mary the Mother of Jesus and the Mother of Christ and the Mother of God. In truth, all these things are the same thing. It is, however, as the Mother of Christ that Mary fully demonstrates the perfection of her acceptance of God's will. As the Mother of Christ she lives constantly with the knowledge that the myrrh given by the Magi will one day be used. Yet she does not rebel or urge her son to shirk His destiny. She trusts completely, even though she knows that as the Mother of Christ she will walk the Way of the Cross with her son. As the Mother of Christ she reveals a perfect trust that God will do the impossible, that He will transform death into eternal life, that He will change her mourning into everlasting joy.

Prayer

Blessed Lady, Mother of Christ and our dearest Mother, hold out the Christ Child to us as you once held Him out to the shepherds and the wise men who came to bask in His glory. Take the little that we have to offer Him and raise it up to His throne in glory and grant that we may one day be with you in the Kingdom of heaven. We ask this in the holy Name of Jesus, Our Lord. Amen.

8
Jesus, Meek and Humble of Heart

> "Come to me, all who labor and are heavy laden, and I will give you rest. Take my yoke upon you and learn from me, for I am gentle and lowly in heart; and you will find rest for your souls. For my yoke is easy, and my burden light."
>
> — Matthew 11:28-30

Have you ever wished, after an encounter with a mean or arrogant person, that you had said something biting in response, that you had been quicker with a rebuke, or somehow gotten the better of that person? These are common feelings, and you are not alone if you held back, if you refrained from insulting and wounding. There are some who just do not use words as weapons. But why did you refrain? It was not dimwittedness that kept you from being nasty. Believe it or not, it was the Christian virtues of meekness and humility that prevented you from lowering yourself to a level where hurting another was your only goal. For the sake of simplicity I will treat these two virtues under the rubric of meekness, which we can say is a virtue that gives us a certain tolerance regarding the faults of others. If you are not proficient in the art of nastiness, you should be pleased, because its opposite — meekness — grows as a result of being virtuous! We may lose points in a fight, but the virtue of meekness gains us blessings even while on this earth. The third beatitude says, "Blessed are the meek, for they shall inherit the earth" (Mt 5:5). That means that we receive blessings right now for dealing well with the faults of others.

Earlier we contemplated Jesus as King of the Universe. Now, we will see a very different aspect of the Son of God. Jesus is described in Scripture and in our Catholic devotional tradition as "meek and humble of heart." I think that the prophet Isaiah describes Our Lord's meekness better than any other writer in the Bible. For Isaiah, the future Messiah will have great care for the vulnerabilities of people: "A bruised reed he will not break, and a dimly burning wick he will not quench" (Is 42:3). In other words, He will treat sinful people with gentleness — how needed in an extremely harsh world. I think my favorite image from Isaiah, though, is this one: "He will feed his flock like a shepherd, he will gather the lambs in his arms, he will carry them in his bosom and gently lead those that are with young" (Is 40:11). Is there a more wonderful image of the meekness of the Lord than His carrying little lambs in His arms and walking side by side with pregnant ewes? I think not.

Yes, Jesus got angry too: All four Gospels show Him expelling the merchants from the Temple with whip in hand and fire in His eyes. But notice that His anger is not vengeful. Apparently, no one was hurt in that incident. Jesus was reestablishing the rights of God in His own Temple, not seeking retribution for those who were doing wrong. Jesus does not prowl around on the lookout for the faults of others. If He did, we'd all be in big trouble. Even in His most emotionally heightened state, He was still meek. He only overturned tables and drove animals away. He did not touch the poorer merchants who were selling doves, but only sent them away with a scolding. That's pretty meek, if you ask me.

Let's look at meekness from a more personal angle, from our own need for it. Have you ever gone to confession and had to choose between whether to go to Father A or Father B? Which priest do you choose to confess your faults to — the stiff, officious, priest with the frown on his face, or the priest who has the face (or at least the reputation) of kindness? Hands down we always choose the priest who looks like he will understand our faults and our weaknesses. But more than anything, we choose the priest who shows in his daily life and preaching that he knows what mercy is and will remind us that God's love is much greater than any sins we could commit. That is the effect that meekness has on people. As a human virtue, it is immensely attractive and trumps nastiness every time.

Most importantly, meekness is that quality of heart that avoids harshness in dealing with the faults of others. It is the attitude that puts up with others' faults patiently, is not contentious in matters that are not essential, and even in difficult moments finds ways of being firm but not mean in dealing with others. How can we survive in this world without meekness? How could we know what true meekness was if the King of the Universe were not also meek and humble of heart?

Prayer

O Jesus, Meek and Humble of Heart, make our hearts like Your own and teach us to be men and women of humble dispositions in all things with all people! Let us never return insult for insult or hatred for hatred. You have given us an example of gentleness and humility, dear Shepherd of our souls. Make our hearts meek and humble so that many souls will draw near to us and walk with us beside the path of life into the Kingdom that you have prepared for all who are meek. Amen.

9

Mary, Our Lady of Mercy

> "Hail, holy Queen, Mother of Mercy,
> our life, our sweetness and our hope.
> To thee do we cry, poor banished children of Eve;
> to thee do we send up our sighs,
> mourning and weeping in this valley of tears."
>
> — From the *Salve Regina*

When I look at certain paintings or statues of our Blessed Mother, I often become aware that I am in the presence of Our Lady of Mercy. This title seems to be a natural designation for her; perhaps it is the most natural of all her many titles. I urge you to sit in prayer before one or another of the great artistic representations of Our Lady. You don't have to be in a famous museum or a cathedral to do this, nor do you have to be in front of a breathtaking Byzantine icon. Gazing at a simple holy card will work just fine. Look deeply into her eyes and contemplate her expression. I can almost guarantee that if you do, you will see mercy given human form. In so many great pictures it seems that mercy radiates from Our Lady as she tenderly holds her infant son, or as she mournfully gathers that same son's lifeless body, broken and battered, into her arms. In such pictures we intuitively understand our Blessed Mother to be Our Lady of Mercy. Even those who have never heard this title before will understand her this way.

Why is that? Why is it that so many people easily see that Mary of Nazareth is truly Our Lady of Mercy? In part, I think, it is because we realize that one who loved so deeply and suffered so greatly will understand our own love and our own sorrow. We have little trouble imagining ourselves held in her gentle arms or being comforted by her soft voice as we face the many trials and disappointments of our lives. We know that she understands us because she has experienced what we experience. Another important reason is that she is our mother, and our first understanding of mercy almost always comes from the woman who has given us life. Motherhood and mercy go hand in hand. In fact, in the Hebrew language, the language in which Mary prayed, the word for mercy is tellingly derived from the word that means "womb." There is no symbol of mercy more powerful than that of a mother tending to a helpless child.

The greatest reason, however, can be found in Our Lady's complete transparency to the will of God. Mary's total acceptance of the Divine will and the Divine love in her life makes her become like a prism. Through that prism, the infinite mercy of God passes absolutely unimpeded, refracting into a thousand brilliant colors and filling our sinful world with a kind of mercy that it doesn't really deserve — except in the eyes of God.

Our Blessed Mother always points us to her Divine Son and through Him to the Holy Trinity, so, when we experience Mary as Our Lady of Mercy, we should never forget that the mercy she shows us is ultimately the mercy of God. We should never forget that when she opens her arms wide to us and then enfolds us in her mantle, she is really offering not simply her own mercy, but a kind of mercy that is beyond any human comprehension, a mercy that is freely given, a mercy that flows from God through our Blessed Mother to give us life and hope, a mercy that — if we accept it — will illumine our souls forever.

Prayer

Holy Mary, Mother of Mercy, you are known by all men as a font of mercy to sinners, and so, with confidence, we turn to you with all our sins and sorrows. Keep us from having to bear the full weight of our many sins, but through your clemency help us always to be instruments of mercy to others. We ask this in the Name of Jesus Christ, Our Lord. Amen.

10

Jesus, Father of the Poor

"The spiritual poverty of the Western world is much greater than the physical poverty of our people. You, in the West, have millions of people who suffer such terrible loneliness and emptiness. They feel unloved and unwanted. These people are not hungry in the physical sense, but they are in another way. They know they need something more than money, yet they don't know what it is."

— Blessed Teresa of Calcutta

I have always wanted to live and work with the poor, and from the time I was in high school, I assumed that such work would be the heart and soul of my vocation as a religious and as a priest. That statement may sound a little strange coming from someone who has lived for nearly four decades in beautiful, exotic Larchmont, New York, near some of the most affluent people in the United States. It is true nonetheless, and, I think it proves that God has a sense of humor — in fact, a pretty good one.

Being a friar in Larchmont has been unusual. You see, I don't blend very well into the local scenery. In fact, I stick out like a sore thumb. My gray Franciscan habit and sandals make me look like something out of *The Canterbury Tales* wherever I go. But in this elegant neighborhood, they make me look like something from a different planet (a planet with a strangely impaired sense of style). Many people have gawked at me as they sped by in cars that cost far more than many others earn in a year. I always smile back, wave, and think that these people have all the things that money can buy, including insulation from many of the unpleasant things of life.

Yet I know that some of the people who drive those expensive cars and live in luxurious homes are poor, poor in ways they might not even comprehend. Certainly their poverty has little in common with that of people in the South Bronx, where so many of the Franciscan Friars and Sisters of the Renewal live and work. Nonetheless, I maintain that some of the people here in Larchmont are very poor, as are some of the richest people in the world, for true poverty does not restrict itself to a mere lack of funds. Poverty can take many forms, and one of the most insidious of those is spiritual poverty. This form of poverty is especially corrosive to the human soul and is especially common in our country. The chronic lack of money can be horrible. It can grind people into the earth. Yet, I have witnessed many people with little money who were happy, even joyful. They had family and friends who loved them, and they possessed a strong, vibrant faith that sustained them. They had hope for the future, whether that hope was for themselves or for their children. They also had the will to go on. All this sprang from a trust in God, in Christ, the Father of the Poor. This trust strengthened them as they confronted the many challenges in their lives.

Those who are spiritually poor, however, lack that strength. Their faith is in their money, in the things they possess, in themselves. All of these, in the end, must fail them. The spiritually poor are often people who have achieved what the world calls success. Yet, their success brings them only a temporary, fragile kind of security, one in constant decay, one that turns into a gnawing emptiness rather than the happiness they expected.

Such people lack nothing, according to the world. But, as is so often the case, the world is absolutely wrong. These people lack everything, for they do not know Jesus, the Father of the Poor. They ignore the only One who can fill the emptiness that consumes their lives. They shun the only One who can offer them riches that will not fade.

As Catholics, I hope we understand what true riches consist of. I hope we know that no matter how poor we have become the Source of all wealth still beckons to us. Jesus, the loving Father of all who are poor, yearns to heal our lives and to banish our poverty forever. Surrender your pride to Him, and you will find that you are also surrendering your poverty. Give Him all that makes your life empty, and the Father of the Poor will fill your life with a joy that knows no end. He will give you riches beyond any imaginings, riches that last for eternity.

Prayer

Dearest Jesus, lover of the poor, father of orphans, and defender of widows, look with compassion upon all who are weak and in need of Your help. Give us the grace we need to live with gratitude for what we have and to be always concerned about those less fortunate than ourselves. We ask this in Your most holy Name. Amen.

11
Mary, Our Lady of Good Counsel

"Mother of Good Counsel, return to us. On the path of peace, lead us."

— From the Devotions to Our Lady of Good Counsel

Good counsel is a rarity in our world. There are far too many competing voices telling us what to do, voices that contradict each other and often speak without love or respect, voices that not only counsel us but demand of us that we act in ways we know to be wrong. At times we might feel as if we've been cast adrift. We live in a world of constantly contending ideas and wildly differing opinions. Liberals hate conservatives, and conservatives despise liberals. It is tragic and perhaps unforgivable that even in the Church this is often the case. Our reluctance to jump on the bandwagon when it comes to ideas that will radically transform the very underpinnings of our culture somehow leaves us vulnerable to charges of bigotry, of hate. Everything seems to be in flux; everything seems to be up for grabs. Nothing is certain.

Yet, we have not been cast adrift. If we can but shut out the din around us for a moment — and the din that also rages in our minds — we might realize in the depths of our souls that God has not retreated from our confusing world. He is still present and will eventually prevail in all things. We should also realize that the counsel we need and search for so desperately has already been given. It is exactly the same as the one counsel that Our Lady offers in all of Scripture.

Do you recall it? Search your memory for a moment. In holy Scripture, Mary is usually shown as observing or pondering. She is so often a figure of contemplation that we tend to forget the one time she offered counsel, the one time she insisted that someone do something she instructed. It is told only in the Gospel of Saint John. It took place during the story of the wedding feast at Cana, at the time when that wedding seemed destined for disaster. The wine had run out, and the guests were clamoring for more. Mary, moved by compassion, implored her Divine Son to help spare the bridal couple the humiliation that seemed inevitable. At first, He seemed to reject her plea almost callously, saying: "O woman, what have you to do with me? My hour has not yet come" (Jn 2:4). But Mary was undaunted, for she knew her son very, very well. "Do whatever He tells you" (Jn 2:5), she instructed the servants. And then all the problems came to an abrupt end.

There it is; in those few words we have Mary's perfect counsel to humanity: "Do whatever He tells you." If the world had followed Our Lady's good counsel we would be in a far better place than we are now. I see no reason to believe that the world will begin to heed Our Lady's words in the near (or even in the far) future, but *we* can heed them. We can remember them whenever we are doubtful and confused, whenever we are deafened by the strident sound of secular voices demanding that we relinquish our morals and our souls. We must try to keep in mind that the path is really simpler than we think, that the words of Our Lady of Good Counsel show us the way with a simplicity that perhaps can only be appreciated fully by the greatest of saints: "Do whatever He tells you." This is the good counsel that holds all the answers.

The Church is with us to fill in the details. In the two thousand years of its existence, the Church has compiled the prayerful writings and thoughts of countless saints, of the Fathers, of the great theologians to help us discern the will of God in various situations. We should turn to all this and learn from it. But the most important thing is the simplest — and also the most difficult. The Gospels constantly point to a way of life that follows what Christ tells us, a way of life that is illustrated most fully in the beatitudes. This is a way of life marked by uncompromising love and generosity, a way of life marked by faith and humility

I urge you to reread the Gospel accounts of the Sermon on the Mount, and to meditate deeply on the beatitudes as they are recorded there. Then, I expect you to follow the advice of Our Lady of Good Counsel. I expect you to try your level best to "do whatever He tells you."

Prayer

Mother of wisdom and Our Lady of Good Counsel, obtain for us the true wisdom of Christ so that we may always have right judg-

ment about the things of this world and loving concern for the world to come. Give us the grace to know God's will and the courage to put it into effect. We ask this in the Name of Jesus Christ, our Lord and God. Amen.

12

Jesus, Angel of Great Counsel

> "The people who walked in darkness have seen a great light;
> those who dwelt in a land of deep darkness, on them has light shined… .
> For to us a child is born, to us a son is given, and the government will be upon his shoulder,
> and his name shall be called 'Wonderful Counselor, Mighty God, Everlasting Father, Prince of Peace.'
> Of the increase of his government and of peace there will be no end."
>
> — Isaiah 9:2,6-7

We read this splendid passage from the Book of Isaiah during the Advent season every year. I never fail to find in it a very real experience of the majesty and awesome dignity of the One whose birth the prophet Isaiah was predicting. The titles that Isaiah uses to describe the future Messiah are unusual and can be translated in several ways from the original Hebrew, but no matter how you translate them, they are magnificent — unique. They remain fixed in our minds because they describe Jesus in ways that are different from those to which we are accustomed. Above all, He is described as "Wonderful Counselor," a title that has come down to us in the Christian devotional tradition as the "Angel of Great Counsel."

What, however, are we to make of this lovely but mysterious title? First, let me explain a little bit of the Hebrew background of the terms, and then we will see what we can discern. The term "angel," when applied to Jesus does not mean that He was an angel in the way Saint Michael is an angel. Jesus is God, pure and simple, and angels are creatures. As the Letter to the Hebrews states, Jesus is "as much superior to the angels as the name he has obtained is more excellent than theirs" (1:4). When we use such a term in reference to our Divine Savior, we use it as an analogy that helps us better understand His role as Savior. You see, in Hebrew, the term "angel" simply means "messenger," and when applied to Jesus it means that He is the first and most important Messenger of God, much the way that a prime minister of a nation is the first and most important minister of government. Jesus is the holy Messenger who came from heaven to reveal God to us in His fullness. Without Jesus there would be no light, truth, or salvation.

"Counsel" is a term with which we are more familiar. We remember it from our confirmation classes. Six out of the seven names for the gifts of the Holy Spirit come from the eleventh chapter of the Book of Isaiah, and "counsel" is one of them. It is commonly mistaken for the word "council," which means a gathering of minds. Yet, "counsel" means more than the ability to consult with a group to get advice. It denotes the ability to guide people to a full understanding of the Truth. Perhaps you remember in the Gospel of John where Jesus calls the Holy Spirit, the "Counselor," and promises that the Holy Spirit would "guide [them] into all truth" (16:13). That is counsel in the best sense. Jesus is called the Messenger of the "Great Counsel," which means that He (through His Holy Spirit) is the One who is uniquely capable of guiding every soul in history to heaven.

I can honestly say that I have met a small handful of greatly gifted individuals whom I think of as geniuses. There are others I know who are enormously talented in one field or another, so talented that I would stake my life on their abilities. Yet, I know that none of them can give me great counsel in its fullest sense. It is not possible for a human being, no matter how gifted, to know everything that needs to be known or to be able to manage all the intricacies of human nature. Only Jesus is Lord of it all. He is the Angel of Great Counsel who is in charge of every aspect of the Father's creation. He is the one who can give us the great counsel that leads to the salvation of our souls. To Him, we owe our total allegiance.

We must ask ourselves whether or not we are open to this supreme Messenger. Can we truly say that we listen to Him, seek His counsel, and make His will our first priority? Do we see Him as the unlimited Lord of our lives and commit ourselves to Him fully? Have we learned to trust Him unreservedly? That is the constant challenge of our journey through life, but the traveling is made easier knowing that we have the Angel of Great Counsel who loves us without limits and has won the right to be our guide to heaven.

Prayer

All-holy Angel of Great Counsel, You have come to be our Lord and guide. Lead us through the trials and tribulations of this life to the joys of heaven. Help us to know what it is You wish of us in every circumstance of our lives and make us instruments in the salvation of the souls of others for the greater honor and glory of God. Amen.

13
Mary, Our Lady of Sorrows

"Rejoice, much sorrowing Mother of God.
Turn our sorrows into joy
And soften the hearts of evil men."

— From the Byzantine prayer to "The Most Holy Mother of God, The Softener of Evil Hearts"

Sorrow is part of every human life. We try to flee from it, and from time to time it may even seem that we can outrun it, but the truth is that sorrow touches every one of us in one way or another. Sorrow at the loss of one we love deeply can be the most devastating sadness. Such sorrow leaves people incapacitated, lost, feeling incapable of going on. Recently, a woman whom I knew ended her life. She was found dead of an overdose of pills, cradling in her arms the picture of her husband of many years. He had died just weeks before. Sorrow had inundated this woman's life to such an extent that she thought that the future could hold nothing for her but pain and loneliness. This is unspeakably sad, because it is not rare. The American poet Emily Dickinson depicts this kind of sorrow in a startling line from one of her poems: "There is a pain so utter it swallows substance up."[4] These words make us uncomfortable because we know them to be true. We know how frail we are, and we know that pain and sorrow can obliterate everything good in our lives.

Yet, we are Catholics, and as Catholics we should see deeply into the true nature of sorrow. We know that no matter how bleak things may seem, there is no sorrow so "utter" that it can swallow up the love of God. We should also never forget that our sorrow has meaning, especially if we unite it with the suffering Christ. "Now I rejoice in my sufferings for your sake, and in my flesh I complete what is lacking in Christ's afflictions" (Col 1:24), writes Saint Paul in one of his most enigmatic statements. It is a statement that powerfully reminds us that suffering and sorrow can be redemptive, can be transformed into something else — even into joy.

4 Emily Dickenson, *The Complete Poems of Emily Dickenson*. ed. Thomas H. Johnson. Boston: Little Brown and Company, 1960, p. 294.

The prophecy of Simeon to Our Lady, that "a sword shall pierce through your own soul" (Lk 2:35), foretold the truth of Our Lady's earthly existence in a devastating way. In the light of this prophecy, her life can be understood as one of sorrows. Hers was a life lived in the shadow of the constantly impending loss of the son she loved with all her being. Event after event seemed to foreshadow this. Her hasty flight into Egypt with Joseph and the Child saved Jesus from the butchery of Herod. Yet, Our Lady must have understood — if only vaguely — that this made possible an even more terrible death at a later time. The disappearance of the young Jesus in the Temple must have been unbearable to her, for even after the boy was found she would know forever what the dread sense of His absence would be like.

And then the moment finally came when sorrow was to envelop her completely, when, as the sorrowing mother, she walked the Way of the Cross with her son. Can we even imagine what it was like for her as she stood beneath the Cross? She was powerless, watching as His life ebbed away, as His lifeless body was placed in her hands, and finally as He was sealed in a tomb, seemingly forever.

Yet, Our Lady was not crushed. She bore her sorrows with faith and grace and as perfect a trust as any human being can have. She knew that even when she could not see beyond her sorrows, God could, and she trusted God to gather all the sorrows of her life and transform them into something beyond her imagination. We know that out of her sorrows, out of the death of her beloved son, new life and new light came into the world. A new creation was born.

We are not like Mary, and our trust is weak. However, we can turn to Mary as Our Lady of Sorrows. We can ask her to be with us when it is our time to walk the Way of the Cross. We can ask for her to comfort us on those occasions when sorrow envelops us completely.

Our Blessed Lady, Our Lady of Sorrows, will never desert us. She will be with us, helping us bear the load of our sadness until the moment when her Divine Son will wipe away every tear from our eyes.

Prayer

O holy Mary, Mother of Sorrows, to you do we turn in every affliction and problem that we face, confident that you will always hear us and provide a remedy for our needs. May we never stray from the Way of the Cross, but love it more and more under your loving guidance and care. We make this prayer in the Name of Jesus our Lord. Amen.

14
Jesus, Healer of Shattered Hearts

"The Lord is close to the brokenhearted,
and saves the crushed in spirit.
Many are the afflictions of the righteous;
but the Lord delivers him out of them all."

— Psalm 34:18-19

I'm going to start this meditation with a small confession: I'm not really sure where this title comes from. It's certainly not part of the Litany of the Holy Name. Nor is it one of the usual titles used for our Divine Savior. I suspect that I read or heard it somewhere, and it just stuck in my mind. If by using it I am inadvertently borrowing the title of somebody else's book, poem, hymn, or prayer, I thank that person. I have decided to include this title because I believe it points us to something of great importance: there are people among us whose hearts have been completely shattered — shattered beyond any earthly repair. Each of us has experienced or will experience a moment when our world seems to disintegrate around us. Most of us are eventually able to pick up the pieces, to re-create our lives in some way and go on. Some people, however, have been so completely devastated that they cannot do this. I believe there are many people in our selfish, fast-paced culture who have been left behind. Thee are forgotten people who live on the edge of despair, people whose lives and hearts are in a million pieces. Often, they are so exhausted and discouraged that they have given up striving or even praying for wholeness. It is these people whom I urge to meditate on this title of our Divine Savior, for I believe that in doing so they may achieve at least a measure of peace and certainly a source of hope.

All that we love in this world can be taken from us in a few moments. Dreams we have cherished for years or even decades can be dashed in an instant. Our health is ephemeral and can evaporate overnight, never to return. There are experiences of loss so intense that they burn forever in our souls, consuming us from the inside out. I am the first to say that there may be no earthly remedy for any of this, but I am also the first to say that we have not been created to be solely of this earth. We must never forget what Jesus, the Healer of Shattered Hearts, shows us: that the power of God is infinite, that the love of God can heal that which the greatest forces of the universe cannot heal. In Jesus Christ we find a cure for all the ills and tragedies of human life, a cure that is offered to us by wounded hands. It is a cure that gushes from the side of a body that was cruelly pierced by a lance. In the Crucified One we find a human life that was shattered even more than we have been shattered — shattered far beyond any earthly repair. In Christ we find a life that the forces of imperial Rome obliterated with overwhelming power; we find One who was horribly betrayed by a trusted friend, betrayed by the religious authorities of His people, and abandoned by those who regularly declared their love for Him. If one reads the Gospel narratives from their beginning to the point at which Jesus is laid in the tomb, we have the perfect — the archetypal — story of the shattered life.

But we know that the Gospels do not end there, and we read on. We read of the infinite love and power of God reaching into a life that mortal eyes saw as being absolutely destroyed — utterly ended. We read of God undoing damage that mortal men know cannot be undone. We read of death, pain, betrayal, and abandonment being turned into their opposites, into life and love, of a resurrected life that is so real, so powerful, that it has transformed the earthly lives of countless people for centuries, and continues to do so today.

The resurrected Jesus is the Healer of the shattered heart, the shattered life. He is the One who proves that our pain, as real and as awful as it may be, is finite and cannot withstand the infinity of the God who loves us with a never-ending love. Jesus is the "first born of the dead" (Col 1:18), but only the first. We who try to follow Him in life are assured that we will follow Him in this as well. All is never lost; the love of God is present in our darkest moments.

If we have the eyes to see them, we will notice that there are a thousand little symbolic resurrections in our lives and in the world around us: the sudden recovery from terrible illness, the healing of broken human relationships, even the coming of spring each year. I urge you to notice these things, and let them speak to you. Let them be a constant reminder of what awaits you: the resurrected life, the life of perfect wholeness, the life that the Healer of Shattered Hearts has opened for you.

Prayer

O merciful Jesus, Healer of Shattered Hearts, no one can walk through life without pain and suffering, but You have walked this way before us, and give us hope to overcome the trials and tribulations of this world. Heal all those who have experienced great loss and strengthen all our hearts to be like Your own most sacred and adorable heart. We ask this in Your most holy Name. Amen.

15

Mary, Mother Most Pure

"Our heart yearns towards that pure Virgin, that gentle Mother,
and our congratulations follow her, as she rises from Nazareth and Ephesus,
through the choir of angels, to her throne on high,
so weak, yet so strong; so delicate, yet so glorious;
so modest and yet so mighty."

— From a letter by Blessed John Henry Newman
to the Rev. E. B. Pusey, D.D.

What is purity? Can we even define it? Is it really even possible for us to imagine it? I suspect that in our difficult and declining culture purity is usually understood in very narrow terms. Many people will say that a person is pure if he or she has simply managed not to sink into the mire of licentiousness that rises like a high tide around us these days. Such an understanding of purity contains real and important truth, but it doesn't come close to telling the whole truth. Neither does it give a hint of the beauty and the depth of real purity — the purity that is exemplified by our Blessed Mother. It is she who is so appropriately invoked as "Mother Most Pure" in the Litany of Loreto.

Quite a few years ago, I read a book by the nineteenth-century Danish Christian philosopher Søren Kierkegaard called *Purity of Heart Is to Will One Thing*. When I first saw that title, I immediately thought of Our Lady. Despite the fact that Kierkegaard's book had nothing to do with her, the title he chose still seems to me (all these many years later) to speak of her. This is because I believe that in Mary's great purity there was a single focus. She willed but one thing: to unite herself as perfectly as possible with the will of God. But she did not simply will it, she abandoned herself to God, accepting anything and everything the Divine Will sent her way. "Behold, I am the handmaid of the Lord; let it be to me according to your word" (Lk 1:38), she says after hearing the terrifying and perplexing news brought to her by the angel Gabriel at the Annunciation. These are words that can be spoken only by one who possesses a pure and undivided heart, a heart that trusts in God.

In the Sermon on the Mount Jesus proclaims: "Blessed are the pure in heart for they shall see God" (Mt 5:8). In this beautiful biblical verse, we encounter the hard truth that those who will ultimately see God are those who have purified themselves of the sins and idols that render us unworthy of being in the Divine Presence. How frightening this verse can be if we take it seriously, for how can any of us claim to be "pure of heart"? We are divided and distracted; we lapse into sin over and over again; we are not only estranged from God but from each other, and even from ourselves. Purity of heart seems like quite a tall order.

Yet our Blessed Mother is always ready to help us in this. She, who was given a unique kind of purity by God, can be our guide as we try to transform our lives and our hearts until we are able to advance in purity. Mary was born without original sin. However, we must never forget that she remained without sin throughout her earthly life, but not because she was incapable of sin. She had free will, just as we do, and with free will comes the capacity to sin, the capacity to turn away from God. She remained sinless because in her great purity of heart she was able to put aside the things that don't really matter and to turn her attention to that which is vital: she willed only to love God, and she willed to do nothing that would separate her from God. We turn from God to a thousand unimportant things, but Mary turned away from the things that were incompatible with the will of God — from all the impurities of sin.

So when we think of Mary's purity, which was constant and unblemished, we should think of her virginity and her chastity, of course. But we should never stop there. We must also think of the purity of her relationship to God, the purity of her desire to follow God no matter what the cost, the purity of her trust in God, even when things seemed incomprehensible or even hopeless. In all these things — indeed, in every aspect of her life — we see a purity that is intense and powerful. We know we can never achieve such purity of heart in our own lives. Yet, we must ask our Mother Most Pure for her prayers as we try, in our own feeble, way to emulate her.

Prayer

Mother Most Pure, holy Virgin of all purity and goodness, transform our bodies and souls to be like yours, pure vessels for the grace of God. Pour out the holy spirit of purity upon us so that we can see God with the eyes of a child and so enter His kingdom. We ask this through our Lord Jesus Christ, in union with the Father and the Holy Spirit, now and forever. Amen.

16

JESUS, PURITY OF VIRGINS

"I am already the spouse of a Lover much more noble and powerful than you. He is a Prince whose bride keeps, as the most glorious of crowns, a spotless virginity.
To this Lover, I have vowed my fidelity."

— From *Acts of the Martyrs*, the words of Saint Agnes as she refused the offer of marriage and was martyred for Christ her spouse, AD 304

The virtue of purity has the greatest relevance for us in today's pleasure-saturated culture. Our society bombards us with impurity, drags immorality into our living rooms, and ridicules those who try to live according to a higher calling. In my many years of working with people who are laboring under these burdens, it has become clear to me that they seek purity because it is a way of knowing God, a spiritual value identified in the Sermon on the Mount as of highest importance. The promise for those who are "pure of heart" is that "they will see God" (Mt 5:8). Not a bad deal for "staying clean," as they say in the Bronx. We call Christ, the Purity of Virgins, not only because He inspires young women to consecrate themselves to a life of virginity in every day and age, but more importantly because He is the font of all purity for everyone.

Now, the consecration of one's whole life, including one's sexuality and the renunciation of marriage for the sake of the kingdom of God, is nothing new to the Church. It is hardly necessary to make mention of the centuries of dedicated service that religious orders of consecrated women have given to the Church in the fields of education and health care. The fact that so many of us can look back on the holy consecrated women who have touched our lives so positively is a testimony to the spiritual impact of virginity on the life of the Church, and on the work of saving souls.

In a wider sense I have always been fascinated by the heroic stories of those men and women throughout history who were aware of the precious gift of purity and were even willing to sacrifice their lives for it. Such stories are powerful in a way we don't often imagine. Saint Maria Goretti (d. July 6, 1902) was murdered at the age of twelve for rejecting the attempts of a young man to violate her chastity. He stabbed her numerous times, and yet, she actually died forgiving him. Her example of Christian love was so powerful that this very same man was eventually converted and was present at her canonization forty-eight years later. Can you think of a story that better shows the power of purity and mercy?

Among the most compelling stories of chastity, though, is that of twenty-two Ugandan martyrs in the late 1800s, all young men who were put to death because they refused a king who wanted to commit homosexual acts with them. They suffered cruel tortures rather than renounce their faith or their chastity. In recent decades Uganda has been the only country in Africa to significantly reduce its horrific AIDS rate. The main tool in this victory has been the promotion of chastity before marriage and fidelity within marriage! Is this a coincidence? I believe we can attribute that astounding success to Uganda's spiritual patrimony of the martyrs who died for purity.

Few of us run the risk of being killed for being chaste, but it is true that everyone who wishes to live a life of purity will suffer for it in this world. Yet, the attractiveness of the ideal of sexual and spiritual purity is still strong, and I believe that we are seeing a rebirth of the vitality of purity after the devastation wrought by the so-called sexual revolution. Single people are responding to the Gospel call to purity in a way that we have not seen in several generations. Let us not forget that married people are also called to be chaste by refusing to allow the impurities of the culture, such as contraception and pornography, to enter into their marriages. I greatly admire couples who follow the Church's teaching on marriage. They often suffer for it, but I know they receive a great blessing from God because of their fidelity.

I have no doubt that each of us strives for purity in mind and body every day. Whatever the temptations we feel toward impurity of any type, body or soul, we can always turn to Christ, the Purity of Virgins. He will give us His grace to overcome these forces. Let us also remember in our prayers those who are losing the battle of purity or who are addicted to impure things: God will not let deny His grace to those who keep fighting the good fight of faith for purity, no matter the cost.

Prayer

Holy and pure Lord of Virgins and saints, imbue us with the grace of purity in body and soul so that we may "see God" as promised by the beatitudes. Let us be examples of purity to others and lead them out of sin into Your marvelous purity for the salvation of their souls in a corrupt age. We ask this in Your most holy Name. Amen.

17
Mary, Virgin Most Renowned

"For he has regarded the low estate of his handmaiden. For behold, henceforth, all generations will call me blessed."

— Luke 1:48

Who is more renowned than our Blessed Mother? Can you imagine any woman in all of history who has been the subject of more paintings, sculptures, or lines of poetry? Can you summon up the name of any queen in either ancient or modern history who is better known or more beloved than Mary of Nazareth? Think of the countless churches — from tiny country chapels to soaring Gothic edifices, such as Notre Dame in Paris — that bear her name. Remember the many religious communities dedicated to her, and the huge number of people who wear the Miraculous Medal and pray the Rosary out of devotion to her. Who can guess at the number of baby girls who have been named for Our Lady throughout the Christian centuries? We even dedicate a month, May, one of the loveliest times of the year, to her, and during it we crown her with roses. Even if you pay attention only to the secular world, Mary is surprisingly present, although if you don't look closely you may not notice her. For example, if you live in Maryland, you live in a state that was named in her honor. If you live in Los Angeles, you live in a city dedicated to Our Lady, Queen of Angels. If you are a gardener, you may line the border of your garden with marigolds — Mary's gold. Truly, Our Lady is the "Virgin Most renowned."

Yet, by the world's standards she was little, almost nothing — a simple peasant woman in ancient Palestine. She should have left no historical trace. The swirling sands of the Middle East should have covered up all memory of Mary of Nazareth many centuries ago. Yet, she is with us constantly and is prayed to by millions. The world wonders how this can be, for what we know of her life is sparse. Even in holy Scripture we read about her only occasionally. The Gospel writers offer us tiny and tantalizing bits and pieces concerning Our Lady. We never see the whole picture in the Gospel when it comes to Mary. But we see enough. We see her great love of God and of her son. We see her trust in God, a trust that is absolute and remains firm no matter what happens. When we read of Mary in the Gospels, we know her to be the virgin and mother who waits patiently in the darkness, confident that the love of God will finally break through like a brilliant sun. Something about this patience, this quiet assurance, opens our hearts, and we find that we love her, that we yearn for her patience, her trust, her ability to wait without losing hope or growing bitter. The quiet, almost still figure of Mary makes us sense a profound and mysterious truth. In her we encounter a life unlike any other. In her we see what should have been; we see what was lost because of sin. Mary shows us the serenity that suffuses a life that is not estranged from God. She shows us a life that cannot be overcome by the tempests and disappointments that buffet us all. In Our Lady we see what we yearn desperately to have and to be but cannot have or be in this earthly life.

Mary, who was chosen by God for the unique honor of giving birth to our Divine Savior, was also chosen to be free of any taint of original sin. As such, hers is the only human life that was lived from beginning to end as God intended a human life to be lived. Mary is the Virgin Most Renowned for a thousand reasons. One of the most important reasons is that in her we see hope. We glimpse our far-distant future, a time when the fire of God's love will have finally burnt away all that is dark in our hearts and souls. Mary shows us what it will be like for us when our estrangement from God — our exile — is finally over. We glimpse in the Virgin Most Renowned a time when the unshakable peace and wholeness that marked Mary's life will at last be ours as well.

Prayer

Dear Virgin Most Renowned, powerful advocate for all who turn to you, look down from the heights of heaven upon our poverty. May we find in you all the inspiration we need to overcome the degrading forces of the world and the strength to live upright lives for the saving of souls and the glory of God. We ask this in the most holy Name of Jesus, Our Lord. Amen.

18

Jesus, King of Glory

"In the beauty of the lilies Christ was born across the sea,
With a glory in His bosom that transfigures you and me:
As He died to make men holy, let us die to make men free,
While God is marching on.
Glory, glory, hallelujah!"

— "Battle Hymn of the Republic," verse 5, Julia Ward Howe, 1862

As we reflect on the title, Jesus, King of Glory, we should note that we have grown accustomed to a secular view of glory. This is largely the result of our entertainment culture, which has filled our lives with stories of heroes and villains for decades now. Yet — and this will shock many of my readers, so be sure you're sitting down before you read another word — I believe that if we look closely enough, we will see that even in its most secular expression, the idea of glory can speak to us of God and of Christ, who is the King of Glory.

The generic story usually goes like this: An evil force appears, threatening destruction; a flawed but essentially good man is the only one who might be able to defeat the wickedness and avert the destruction, but he is aware that he may lose his life in the process. (There may actually be a group of heroes, but the good-versus-evil dynamic is the same.) In the ensuing battle, the hero suffers great losses, but eventually vanquishes the danger. Those he was trying to protect are safe. This scenario has been played out over and over again since the early days of movies in stories like *Ben Hur* right up to the more recent dramas like *The Hunger Games.* If I were you, I wouldn't expect this familiar plot to go away an time soon.

What is it about this recurring narrative pattern that never gets old? How is it that such a predictable plot remains eternally popular? The answer, I believe, can be found deep in the human heart, in the relationship of God to His world. It has to do with God's glory.

The good-versus-evil story (with the ultimate victory of the good) reflects the story of God's love for man. Love and freedom go together in God's world, and when God created free creatures like angels and men, He took the risk that they would use their freedom for selfish ends — and they did. That could have been the end of God's love story, but it was not. In God's creation, evil doesn't win in the end because the same love that created His children is strong enough to redeem them through sacrifice, the greatest expression of love.

Because of this, God himself becomes the first hero who comes to save His people from the preternatural forces of evil and destruction. He takes on our flawed human nature and through patience, suffering, heroic deeds, and self-sacrifice buys back His loved ones from the power of annihilation that has come upon them. In other words, God himself established the first template of the hero movie with His own real-life battle and sacrificial death. Every secular hero, every rescue story that was ever told, is just a repeat of that first dramatic love story that ends in ultimate victory. Good conquers evil, and the world is transformed.

Glory is what happens when arms have been laid down, the innocent have been saved, and the victor looks out over the destruction and proclaims that his sacrifice was all worth it. Glory isn't a good feeling or something that can be bought. It is the result of a battle that can only be won at a great cost.

All glory in this world is a tiny reflection of that one unconditional victory. Think of all the heroic figures you have ever read about, or seen on the silver screen, or known in real life, and contemplate one essential truth: Jesus is the King of them all. He is the greatest of all heroes, and the unconditional King of Glory! In an absolute sense, no one has engaged a greater battle, suffered more, conquered a fiercer foe, or given more for his cause than Jesus. He is the supreme hero because He is God, and His victory shows the total primacy and power of His love for His children. In the Gospel of Saint John, He even says that the Father "glorified" Him (17:4) by sending Him to the cross for us. A moment's contemplation of this truth should leave us in utter awe of our Divine Savior.

Prayer

Dearest Jesus, King of Glory, and victor over sin and death, fortify our hearts with Your grace as we fight the earthly battles that we must confront on our way to heaven. Make us know that the victory has already been won and give us hope to experience the glory of the saints in eternal happiness. Amen.

19
Mary, Mirror of Justice

> "For she is the reflection of eternal light,
> the spotless mirror of the working of God,
> and an image of his goodness."
>
> — Book of Wisdom 7:26

This title of our Blessed Mother can seem a mystery. What are we to make of Mary as a Mirror of Justice? To find out, I urge you to imagine a mirror, a perfect, shiny, and spotless one. In such a mirror there are no distortions; what is reflected is reflected perfectly. If Jesus is called the Sun of Justice, then Mary is the perfect reflection of that Sun and its light to others. In this I am reminded of some words of that great Marian saint, Louis Marie de Montfort: "She is so intimately united with Thee that it were easier to separate the light from the sun, the heat from the fire; nay, it were easier to separate from Thee all the angels and the saints than the divine Mary, because she loves Thee more ardently and glorifies Thee more perfectly than all the other creatures put together."[5] What a profound thought. Mary is the perfect reflection of Jesus. In bringing forth the Sun of Justice she has magnified the Sun's light for the entire world to see.

Mirrors also enable us to see things about ourselves that we can't otherwise see, to see ourselves as we appear to others. We cannot see our own faults and failings the way God and other people see them. Mary very gently reflects them to us for our own spiritual benefit, as hard as it may sometimes be to face our true selves.

I remember the story of a young man who was basically decent, but very self-centered and ambitious. Everyone was afraid to point these faults out to him. He chose the legal profession as the quickest way to achieve his personal goals and soon gained the reputation of being a cutthroat lawyer who cared only about money. One day, he fell in love with a beautiful young woman and wanted to marry her. Part of the reason he was attracted to her was that he thought a beautiful wife would enhance his position in the world and get him into certain social circles to which he had no other access. Yet, he was

5 Saint Louis De Montfort, *True Devotion to Mary*, tr. Fr. Frederick Faber, TAN Books and Publishers, Inc.: Rockford, IL, 1985, p. 39.

suspicious by nature, so, without disclosing his real intent, he hired a private detective to look into her background and tell him what negatives she had that might reflect poorly on him. Well, an unexpectedly shocking report came back after a few weeks. The detective told him, "This woman has an impeccable record in every respect. She comes from a good family, has an excellent education, is entirely moral, and has a spotless reputation for charity and goodness. The only black mark on her record is that she has been seen recently with a disreputable young lawyer whom people think is beneath her in every way."

This young man had a good look into a "Mirror of Justice" at that moment. Yet, the reflection of his bad character back to him was both just in the sense that he deserved it, and merciful in the sense that seeing the truth about himself did not totally crush him. We hope the news led him to conversion and some sort of change in behavior.

Our blessed Lady is so close to Jesus that she sees everything through His eyes. She will not change the order of His Justice, but she will help us to live up to it and strive for greater virtue by helping us to see our deeds and character rightly. She is a spotless mirror and will never give a false impression. Mary just wants us to be totally pure and converted in heart so that we can enter into the life of heaven that God has planned for us.

If you are like most people (myself included), you will probably hesitate a moment before asking Mary to reflect back to you the things in your life that need to be changed. It is never easy to see our faults, but we should never fear Mary as she looks lovingly into our lives. As the Mirror of Justice, she reflects the good as well as the bad, and she encourages us to follow the path to her Divine Son. Let us ask the Mirror of Justice today to help us to be fully converted to God and so reflect the light of Christ to others in this world.

Prayer

Heavenly Mother and Mirror of Justice, open our hearts to the light of God's countenance. Shine that merciful light upon our darkness so that we can accept the Gospel message in the depths of our being and enter more fully into the life of heaven. We ask this through the grace and mercy of our Lord Jesus Christ, who lives and reigns forever and ever. Amen

20
Jesus, Sun of Justice

> "He has showed you, O man, what is good; and what does the Lord require of you but to do justice, and to love kindness, and to walk humbly with your God?"
>
> — Micah 6:8

You may notice the play on words which occurs when this title of our Divine Savior is translated into English from the original Latin of the Litany of the Holy Name. The meaning seems to be enhanced and our understanding of this title made deeper. He is both the *Son* of God and the *Sun* of Justice. The sun, as the nearest star in our sky, dominates all other lights, giving warmth and nurturance to all, bringing clarity and color to our world. We need the sun for life and light; without it we would simply shrivel up and die. That is even more the case with our need for justice. Justice is one of the four cardinal virtues from Greek philosophy (prudence, justice, temperance, fortitude), but more importantly, it is a biblical concept which has to do with our relationships with God and man. When we call Jesus the "Sun of Justice" we are really saying that He shines down upon, sustains, and nourishes all of our relationships, both human and divine.

My first exposure to justice in the human sense came from my old Jewish neighbors who were so much a part of my world in Jersey City when I was a boy. They may not have realized it, but they were great teachers when it came to justice. You could be of a different religion or have a difference of opinion with them — and they would fight you about the details — but they would respect you if you had religious faith and didn't do anything dishonest toward them. But if you were a *shyster* — that is, if you stole or cheated or lied in your dealings with them — you were out on your nose in a minute. They had a sense of justice that was very human and very concrete. It came directly from the Old Testament sense of righteousness before God and man, and it meant you had to live up to a higher standard. It also meant you could be judged for failing to live up to that standard. They were tough old birds, but they really taught me about standing on my own two feet and keeping in good with my neighbor.

Of course, in an absolute sense, justice means being able to stand before God with a clean conscience and not demand that God change the order of existence just to suit our own preferences. It means having a certain attitude of humility toward reality. It also means a recognition that God's law runs the world and an understanding that this law enables us to find peace with others and with the world around us. Part of God's law is a moral code that we must live by, one we cannot arbitrarily toss away when it is inconvenient. The reason why the scales of justice are the image of the legal profession is because, in the Final Judgment, we will all be "weighed in the scales" to find out if we have lived up to that code. Certain biblical passages about this judgment are a bit disconcerting to the modern relativistic mind, and 2 Corinthians 5:10 is one of them. It states that "we must all appear before the judgment seat of Christ, so that each one may receive good or evil, according to what he did in the body."

We need not fear judgment, though, if we are devoted to Jesus Christ, the Sun of Justice. He is a merciful judge and also the great teacher of justice for all who wish to learn how to live rightly. First and foremost, Jesus teaches us the difference between right and wrong, fundamental categories of good and evil, the stark difference between justice and injustice. We should always ask Him for guidance in answering the difficult moral questions of our day. When we are in doubt, we need only look to His Church for that guidance. He established His Church to hand on His truth and help men form their consciences rightly.

Second, the Sun of Justice shows us how to maintain proper relationships with people in this world. Would you believe that He is concerned about all relationships from marriages to business partnerships to friendships? If we make Him the Lord of all our relationships, we will always walk in righteousness. That is a biblical way of saying that we receive the blessing of a happy and healthy life and stay on good terms with friend and foe alike. We should seek that blessing from the Sun of Justice with all our hearts.

Last, let us ask the Lord to teach us how to put God first in our lives and in everything we do. That is true justice. The sun is the leading light in the sky, and as the earth revolves around it, so our lives should revolve around Christ, the Sun of Justice. That is the first and essential formula for being just: "But seek first his kingdom and his righteousness, and all these things shall be yours as well" (Mt 6:33).

Prayer

Holy Sun of Justice, Jesus Christ, give balance and clarity to all our relationships, human and divine. Help us always to put the concerns of God's kingdom first so that He will pour out the blessings of His life upon us, and may we live in the peace that surpasses all understanding. Amen.

21

Mary, Refuge of Sinners

> "Remember, O most gracious Virgin Mary, that never was it known that anyone who had fled to thy protection, implored thy help, or sought thy intercession, was left unaided. Inspired by this confidence, we fly unto thee, O Virgin of virgins our Mother; to thee do we come, before thee we stand, sinful and sorrowful. O Mother of the Word Incarnate, despise not our petitions, but in thy mercy hear and answer us. Amen."
>
> — The *Memorare*

How beautiful and consoling is the familiar prayer the *Memorare*, which reminds us that "never was it known" that Mary would refuse help to her children in need. And this really is the basic reality: We are all sinners of Adam's stock, and Mary truly is the Refuge of Sinners who comes to our aid when we get ourselves into messes — and we manage to get ourselves into some major messes! Perhaps we are inclined to think that Mary's sinlessness would entitle her to sit in judgment on sin — on *our* sin! This seems logical, but the Church's experience of Mary is exactly the opposite! She is not the judge of sin but the place of safety for sinners. She is never the accuser (that is the devil's role); she is the ever-loving protector of the accused. Her loving, merciful embrace gives us hope for reconciliation with God. Hope indeed is what sinners find in her sanctuary.

I discovered the logic of this Marian title in a rather strange and unexpected place — the Old Testament. Several of the early books of the Bible (Numbers, Deuteronomy, Joshua) include passages describing the cities of refuge in Israel. It was an amazing discovery for me to realize that God had designated certain cities where people guilty of unintentional manslaughter could find protection from those who were seeking retribution under the old law of "an eye for an eye, and a tooth for a tooth." God, in His mercy, provided protection for those who had sinned. He shielded them from the full consequences of their sin in a city of refuge.

In the New Testament, Jesus is the ultimate expression of God's mercy for sinners, but He is also the judge of the living and the dead. It is He who will execute divine judgment at the end of time for all sins. In Mary, however, Christians sense no trace of judgment, no trace of what the human heart interprets as harshness. We have always recognized her generous love toward sinners. Mary is for us a "city of refuge." We can always run to her and be assured of being accepted, no matter what we have done.

In my years of counseling people in the most desperate circumstances, many suffered tremendously from the consequences of their own actions. I have found that Mary's love gives people a great sense of hope. She enables them to believe that there is a way out of their problems, even desperate problems of their own making. The reality of human life is that we all have an amazing capacity to sink our own boats! And on top of that, we live with the devil's accusatory voice ringing in our ears constantly telling us that we are beyond redemption, that we have no hope, that we are too bad to deserve mercy or love.

That moment of desperation, that place of despair, is where Mary is most powerful. She enters our lives, providing a safe refuge from the devil's warfare on our souls. He is the avenger who shows no mercy. But Mary is the loving mother who undoes his malice. Using the key of our repentance, she opens the door to the narrow pathway leading to heaven. She bestows upon us the hope of finding the way back to God and to her Divine Son.

It is certainly true that God will forgive anyone who turns to Him in sincerity, but it is also consoling for the sinner to know that he has a loving advocate who will bring him to God under her protective mantle. Of course, Mary never endorses sin, nor does she excuse or justify it as we often try to do. But she overshadows human sinfulness with her indulgent love and mercy. She will receive anyone who is truly repentant, under any circumstances, at any time. She will lead them to her son and to eternal life.

Let us run to the marvelous refuge that God has prepared from the foundation of the world for His sinful children. There is no shameful act or secret too terrible to bring to Our Lady. She will not condemn; she will be the refuge to which we may fly, time and time again. In the arms of Our Lady, the Refuge of Sinners, we will discover the power of a mother's tender mercy.

> *Turn then, most gracious advocate, thine eyes of mercy toward us, and after this our exile, show unto us the blessed fruit of thy womb, Jesus.*
>
> *O clement, O loving, O sweet Virgin Mary!*

Prayer

> *Merciful Mother, full of gentle love for sinners, allow us to take refuge in the fold of your mantle where we will find protection from evil and from the judgment that our own sins bring upon us. Help us always to imitate your mercy so that we may bring other sinners to enjoy the peace of heaven. We ask this through your son, Jesus Christ, Our Lord. Amen.*

22

Jesus, Example of Virtue

"Plant deep within us, Lord, all the virtues, that we might be devout in divine matters, discerning in human affairs, and burdensome to no one in fulfilling our own bodily needs."

— *Prayer to Acquire the Virtues*, Saint Thomas Aquinas

When we call Jesus the "Example of Virtue" we do not mean that He was simply a supremely virtuous man or even a holy prophet. Nor do we mean that He is the one who has so much virtue that He parcels it out to His saints. This term means that He *is* Virtue. All virtue flows from Him and finds its perfect expression in Him. He is the source of every goodness in heaven and on earth, and the standard by which all virtue can be judged. Even the cumulative holiness of all the saints — including the Virgin Mary — is nothing more than a spark from the raging bonfire of Christ's life. It would be impossible for us to attain any virtue at all if He did not generously share His virtue with all who ask. More than even the greatest saints, the Lord Jesus inspires us to love virtue and gives us the grace to attain it in our lives. If staying close to truly virtuous people makes us want to be more virtuous, then closeness to Jesus makes us want to be Christ-like in virtue. That is the comprehensive meaning of the title of our Divine Savior that we are now considering: Example of Virtue.

Those of us who have tried to develop virtue[6] in our souls know how very difficult that project can be. The pagan philosophers used to say that if you want to know what virtue is, you only need to find a virtuous man to teach you. I have met thousands of truly virtuous people in my life and have learned virtue from these models more than from any book. Nothing gives us as full a picture of virtue as a living, breathing, virtuous person standing right in front of us and showing us the way to live. If "a picture speaks a thousand words," then surely a virtuous life teaches a thousand lessons. Because the virtues come from God,

6 In the short space available to me here, it would impossible to describe the whole scheme of theological, cardinal, and moral virtues of the Christian life. If you are interested in that, you may wish to look at *The Virtue Driven Life*, a book of mine that was published by Our Sunday Visitor in 2006.

we naturally learn from virtuous people even without their trying to show us anything. Their virtue teaches us *how* to be virtuous. We are naturally "programmed" by God to follow their example.

Allow me to give an example of what I am getting at. Years ago I had the immense privilege of knowing Bishop James Walsh, of Maryknoll. As a missionary to China he had been imprisoned by the Japanese during World War II, and then by the Chinese communists after they took over. All in all, he languished in Asian prisons for almost two decades. He could so easily and understandably have been bitter and angry about what he suffered. In fact, most people would expect such a reaction. Yet, Bishop Walsh would never speak an uncharitable word about another person — including his tormentors! The changes that took place at his beloved Maryknoll after the Second Vatican Council distressed him terribly. But his critiques or comments were always charitable and directed at ideas, never toward people. I often wondered how it was possible for a man to have such a spotless record of never speaking a harsh word about anyone — a record I certainly cannot hope to match. Despite my inability to imitate him well, the charity that exuded from him overflowed into my soul because he showed me exactly what true Christian charity — what real Christ-like charity — looks like. Despite my own deficiency in this virtue, knowing him made me want to be more charitable every day. I'm still working at it.

Virtue is the substance of good living and the essence of Christianity. Are you struggling to live a virtuous life? Are there virtues you need in order to manage a difficult situation? Let us not hesitate to ask Jesus Christ for everything we need! If I could be so bold, I would say that Jesus' greatest virtue is His desire to share all virtue with those who ask.

Prayer

O heavenly Source of everything that is good, Jesus Christ, Example of Virtue, grant to us the overwhelming grace of virtue and the desire to live as You have asked. Give to our virtue the radiance of the saints so that we may touch many souls and lead them to Your kingdom where You live with the Father and the Holy Spirit, forever and ever. Amen.

23

Mary, Queen of Angels

> "A thousand angels were equipped for her guard and custody that they might serve as most faithful vassals of their Queen and Lady."
>
> — Venerable Mary of Agreda, from *Life of the Virgin Mother of God*

The above beautiful thought was taken from a private revelation. It concerns the number of guardian angels that were assigned by God to protect the Virgin Mary during her earthly life. It is by no means dogma, and there is no reason to believe it literally. It may be nothing more than a beautiful and poetic image, but it *is* beautiful, and I personally like to imagine that the Virgin Mary had a thousand guardian angels accompanying her on her journey through life. Venerable Mary of Agreda described this cohort of angels as being made up of one hundred from each of the nine choirs of angels. Added to these were "twelve others who should in a special manner assist Mary in corporeal and visible form," and "eighteen other angels, selected from the highest ranks," and "seventy seraphim, choosing them from the highest ranks and from those nearest to the Divinity." Such an entourage is a little confusing to read about, but it certainly would be most fitting for a queen — especially the exalted Queen of Heaven! It is not hard to see why Mary has become known in the Christian tradition as the Queen of Angels. Think of the many examples in Christian iconography in which she is surrounded by holy angels in heaven.

As modern Americans, we are not accustomed to royalty. In fact, we have very little imagery in our national consciousness to make us monarchists in heart or mind. Yet, in a certain sense, as Christians we have to adapt our thinking to the idea that we really do have a queen in heaven. She plays a dynamic role in the affairs of all the subjects of the realm, with the souls that God wishes to be with Him in heaven.

As queen, Mary commands the angels to do what is necessary for the salvation of souls. Whether she has one thousand guardian angels of her own or not, she has literal command over multitudes of angels in heaven. They understand their role as servants of God's mysterious plan in union with the desires of their queen. There could only be one human mother of the Redeemer of mankind, Jesus Christ. The angels knew that when she was finally revealed in time, she would bear the authority of her son. So, now, they take orders from her as powerful spirits under authority, servants of the grand plan of salvation, as loving caretakers of souls about which Mary is so intimately concerned.

Mary loves the angels because of their fidelity to God, and they love her tenderly and fervently in return. They are pure as she is pure. Their virtue and strength are reflections of her own, and their desire for the glory of God and the salvation of souls burns as deeply in them as it does in Mary, who proclaimed from the beginning, "My soul magnifies the Lord, and my spirit rejoices in God my savior" (Lk 1:46-47).

When we think of Mary as Queen, let us remember that she is queen of many things, but, first of all, she is the Queen of Angels, those firstborn creatures of God who work with Mary to help us on the road to heaven. If the angels sing to God the Church's refrain of *Sanctus, Sanctus, Sanctus!* ("Holy, Holy, Holy!"), then we can sing with the angels the Church's familiar hymn, "Hail Holy Queen," in praising Mary as the Queen of Angels and saints:

> "Cry out, all ye Cherubim! Sing with us, ye Seraphim! Heaven and earth resound the hymn
>
> Salve! Salve! Salve, Regina!"

Prayer

Holy Mary, Queen of Angels and inspiration of saints, send the holy angelic servants of Christ to give us assistance in the trials and tribulations of this life and command them to lead us from all worldly pleasures to the joys of God's kingdom where Jesus lives and reigns, forever and ever. Amen.

24
Jesus, Joy of Angels

> "For to what angel did God ever say:
> 'Thou art my son; today I have begotten thee'?
> Or again: 'I will be to him a father, and he shall be to me a son'?
> And again, when he brings the first-born into the world,
> he says:
> 'Let all God's angels worship him.'"
>
> — Hebrews 1:5-6

We don't think too much about angels in our materialistic age, but every now and then a question concerning them arises to pique our curiosity. The other day I was listening to a call-in radio show on a religious station. One of the callers said that he had heard a story about the fall of Lucifer which he found hard to believe. He asked if the archangel Lucifer fell because he was jealous that Jesus was chosen to be the Messiah instead of him.

The answer to the man's question is simple and should be obvious: Jesus is the eternal God and is not in competition with Lucifer for anything. It was Jesus' eternal vocation to be the Savior of mankind. No one, including Lucifer, ever had a shot at the job. The Evil One is not jealous of Jesus so much as he is jealous of us, because we can accept the salvation that Jesus offers. It was an offer that Lucifer tragically rejected, but we know that there were faithful angels who accepted that offer of eternal happiness and now worship Jesus as their King and their greatest joy.

Why, specifically, is Jesus the Joy of Angels? There are enough reasons to fill a whole book, but let's start with Scripture. First of all, the Gospel of Matthew tells us that the angels "behold the face of my Father who is in heaven" (18:10). We humans hope for that bliss at the end of our lives, but the angels already possess it. Tradition tells us that when the holy angels remained faithful, they entered into what we call the Beatific Vision and now live with eternal joy in God's presence. I think that if I were constantly beholding the face of God, I would be totally joyful too. I can only hope and pray that my moment of joy will come — after I do my time in purgatory, of course.

Jesus is the Joy of Angels because they participate with Him in His grand plan of salvation. Imagine this: the greatest of all heroes, the most supreme of all commanders, the highest of all leaders, and the bravest of all warriors calls the angels into His service to dedicate themselves to the noblest of all causes — the salvation of souls. Except for their role in worshipping God, the angels exist for no other reason than to get man to heaven. The Letter to the Hebrews says rather sedately that the angels are "ministering spirits sent forth to serve, for the sake of those who are to inherit salvation" (1:14). What a wonderful, joyful work that is for them! Maybe you have felt a similar joy and exhilaration when you embarked upon your vocational path and knew that God had chosen you for some important work such as marriage, religious life, or a meaningful career. Maybe you felt that joy when you first laid eyes on a newborn baby or helped a friend overcome some great difficulty. You experienced joy as a natural emotion that resulted from doing God's work and partaking in His greatest blessings. The angels experience that joy constantly as they see God's plan mysteriously unfolding in the salvation of His children.

Finally, Jesus is the Joy of Angels because they were the ones who escorted Him into heaven after His mission was accomplished on earth. Their joy must have known no bounds. Scripture imagines the angels crying out at that moment: "Sing to God, sing praises to his name … his name is the Lord, exult before him" (Ps 68:4). The rejoicing at the Ascension will be surpassed only by the rejoicing at the end of time when Jesus will come back to put an end to sin, death, and the power of the devil forever.

Let us learn a lesson from the holy angels who find their greatest joy in Jesus. If the obligations of our faith are burdensome at times, let us trust that the deepest dimension of the Christian faith is the joy that knows no bounds. It is the joy that comes from living fully for God and working our hardest to get ourselves and others to heaven. When we finally get there, we will experience the fullness of joy, just as the angels do, because we will finally behold the King face to face.

Prayer

Jesus, Joy of Angels and men, open our hearts to the angelic joy which surpasses all understanding and to the love that You so lavishly pour out from Your Most Sacred Heart. Send Your holy angels to assist us in this life, and lead us safely to the life to come. Amen.

25
Mary, Cause of Our Joy

"Shout for joy, O daughter Zion! Sing joyfully, O Israel!
Be glad and exult with all your heart, O daughter Jerusalem!
The Lord has removed the judgment against you; he has turned away your enemies.
The King of Israel, the Lord, is in your midst, you have no further misfortune to fear."

— Zephaniah 3:14-15 [7]

What a beautiful title this is! I really think it is my favorite of all Marian titles because the one thing that this wretched world desperately needs is joy. I'm sure you'll agree with me when I say that we have more than enough suffering to go around. Even when things are good, we know deep in our hearts that the world can come crashing down around us in seconds. "There's gotta be a better way!" I often say (with tongue more or less in cheek). But I mean those words because I am at a time in my life when I really feel the aches and pains of age, the uncertainties of life. It gives me great comfort and happiness to know that Mary has actually given us that better way. She has given us the Joy of Angels and a way for the whole world to be our very own. There is no greater joy in heaven or on earth than the son she gave us.

If we call to mind just a few of the Scripture passages that describe Mary's early life, we will see joy all over the place. The jubilant angels sang in the night sky of Bethlehem when the Christ Child was born. Two millennia later we sing, "Joy to the World!" and "Hark the Herald Angels Sing!" in commemoration of the eternal joy that entered the world that night. When Mary went in haste to the hill country of Judea, her cousin Elizabeth exclaimed, "For at the moment the sound of your greeting reached my ears, the infant in my womb leaped for joy" (Lk 1:44). Joy seems to accompany Mary wherever she goes!

The psalmist asks God to "make us glad as many days as you humbled us, for as many years as we have seen trouble" (Ps 90:15). That is the perennial cry of the human heart. But is it really possible for us to find joy amidst all the sorrowful mysteries of our lives? I be-

7 In this chapter Scripture quotations are from *The New American Bible*

lieve that is what Mary teaches us most beautifully. She does not come to take away the sufferings of this world — I often wish she would — but rather, she helps us find joy, peace, and tranquility despite and within those sufferings so that we can transform them into prayer.

I can think of many saintly priests whom I have had the pleasure of knowing who witness that joy is possible, even within suffering. I met the saintly Father Walter Ciszek, S.J., some years after he was released from his twenty-three-year sojourn in Siberian prison camps. Imagine being in Communist prison camps for almost a quarter of a century! Father was arrested on trumped-up charges that he was a "Vatican spy," but after his initial rebellion against the atheistic communist system, he accepted his trials as God's way of purifying him and bringing him closer to Christ and his fellow man. Rarely have I seen a man more in tune with the Spirit of Christ and the joy that lies beneath the surface of all sufferings.

In his remarkable book, *He Leadeth Me*, Father Ciszek explains where he found strength and joy amidst his sufferings: "Mass and the Blessed Sacrament were … the source of my strength and joy and spiritual sustenance. But it was when I realized what the Holy Eucharist meant to these men, what sacrifices they were willing to make for it that I felt animated, privileged, driven to make it possible for them to receive this bread of life as often as they wished. No danger, no risk, no retaliation could prevent my saying Mass each day for them."[8] This holy man, tested to the extreme, found the depths of joy in so much suffering.

Truly, joy is everywhere in the world if we look for it. As Christians we don't have to look very far. Our Mother Mary is here with us and bestows that spiritual joy on any who ask. Sometimes it is in the consolation of humor or the deep beauty of a child. At other times, joy is found in the embrace of suffering for others and the cleansing of one's soul. Whatever the source in this world, we can look to Mother Mary as the Cause of Our Joy because she has lavished upon us the greatest Joy of all, Christ, the Joy of the entire world. Christ's love conquered sin, suffering, and even death.

---

8 Walter J. Ciszek, S.J., *He Leadeth Me* (Garden City, New York: Doubleday, 1973), p. 132.

Prayer

Mother of our souls and Cause of Our Joy, graciously fill our lives with the joy of knowing Christ, and let that joy flow over into a world tainted by sin and evil. May our joy scatter the forces of darkness around us and lead us safely into the Kingdom of Joy in the world to come. We ask this through Christ our Lord. Amen.

26

Jesus, the Good Shepherd

> "For thus says the Lord God: Behold I, I myself will search for my sheep …
> As a shepherd seeks out his flock … so will I seek out my sheep …
> and I will bring back the strayed, and I will bind up the crippled, and I will strengthen the weak."
>
> — Ezekiel 34:11,16

First of all, let's forget about those sentimental pictures of Jesus as the Good Shepherd which we have all been subjected to since childhood. I'm sure you know the ones I mean. They depict a very calm and gentle Jesus — sometimes a passive or even effeminate Jesus — surrounded by cute and fleecy white lambs in a lush green meadow. Often, He is shown holding one of the smallest lambs, almost cradling it in His arms as one would a child. It is a bucolic scene absolutely devoid of drama, conflict, and uncertainty. And it has very little to do with what our Divine Savior meant when He called himself our "Good Shepherd."

Let us think about what things were really like for shepherds in the Holy Land at the time of Jesus' earthly life. First of all, there were no lush, green meadows in that land of intense summer heat and dryness. Not until modern Israeli irrigation techniques came into being in the middle part of the last century did Palestine begin to bloom. Before that the climate and rough terrain would have made herding sheep difficult and uncertain. Such work was the task of nomads, people who were far down on the social scale. They had to be in constant motion with their flocks in search of the scant water and vegetation that offered continued life. Shepherding meant forfeiting a home and family for the sake of the flock. It meant sleeping outside at night, lying on the ground in front of the open entrance to the sheepfold. It meant becoming a living barrier to all who wanted to stray and to all who wanted to enter and destroy. It meant standing alone against thieves as well as any of the many predators who would consider sheep to be easy and tasty prey. As if all this were not bad enough, the sheep were dusty and dirty, not very smart, and they probably didn't smell very good either.

So, it seems that the symbol of the shepherd has little that is beautiful about it. It seems to be an unworthy image for the incarnate Son of God. Yet, Jesus refers to himself repeatedly as our Good Shepherd, and of His many titles, this one resonates with people more deeply than most. Why is this? I believe it is because we occasionally see ourselves as we really are. In those rare moments we understand that we are more like those sheep in ancient Palestine than we usually care to admit. Despite our pride and arrogance, we understand that in many ways we are helpless and even hopeless. We cannot care for ourselves fully; we cannot guide ourselves through the twists and turns of life in search of the sustenance we need to survive. Given half a chance we know that we will bypass the next oasis, following one desert mirage after another, until we are hopelessly lost in the wilderness.

In the image of the Good Shepherd, however, we know we have found One upon whom we can depend, One who will go in search of us when we are lost and will care for us no matter what happens. We know that this Shepherd's concern is not just for His flock but for each of us individually. He knows our names, our problems, and our weaknesses. We are all sadly aware that we are capable of alienating our families and those people who call themselves our friends, of making them give up on us. But the Good Shepherd never gives up on us; for Him no sheep is ever truly lost. We derive hope from His promise to follow us no matter how far we stray. We rejoice over His willingness to pursue us through the arid wastes of our life. We derive joy from the knowledge that He will carry us home on His strong shoulders. We derive peace from knowing that He does all this because He sees our worth even when we cannot. He knows we are worthy of love, even when we have ceased to believe it.

Prayer

Heavenly Shepherd of our souls, watch over us and protect us from the wolves that seek to destroy us. Keep us safe within the confines of Your Church. May Your rod and staff give us courage to make our way through the valley of the shadow of death into the life of heaven. We ask this in Your most holy Name. Amen.

27

Mary, Our Lady of Perpetual Help

"Most holy and Immaculate Virgin and our Mother Mary,
you are our Perpetual Help,
our refuge and our hope."

— Mother of Perpetual Help devotions

Let us begin this meditation by focusing not on Our Lady, herself, but on two of the words contained in this wonderful title. Let us look at the word "help" and the word "perpetual." Say them slowly to yourself a few times, and contemplate their meaning. If you do, I am sure a feeling of gratitude will begin to flow through you, for these words offer us an enormous amount of hope and encouragement. As we begin to comprehend the meaning of these words, we realize that a great gift has been given to us by God through our Blessed Lady and through the saints, as well. It is a gift that can never fail us.

As Catholics we are blessed in too many ways to count. We are never truly alone in our struggles, in our joys, in our sadness. We do not have to face anything by ourselves without help, and we certainly do not have to make the journey to God on our own. We are part of the Body of Christ, intimately bound to countless others. We are surrounded by a great "cloud of witnesses" (Heb 12:1) who care for us and pray for us unceasingly. We are never left to our own devices, for we have the perpetual help of Our Lady — and not only of Our Lady, but of the entire Body of Christ.

I believe that many people understand this on some level, even if they are not able to express it in words. I believe it because of the popularity of the icon that is the source of the title "Our Lady of Perpetual Help." This Byzantine icon, so different from the religious art most of us grew up with, is probably the most famous and recognizable icon among Western Catholics. Devotion to it has permeated the entire Western Church; no other Eastern icon has received that type of response.

Think of the icon of Our Lady of Perpetual Help, which depicts Mary holding her Divine Son. Remember that one sandal dangles from the foot of the Christ Child. Remember also that two angels are in the upper corners of the icon bearing the symbols of the Passion. Tradition suggests that at this reminder of His painful future, the Child ran in terror to his mother, ran so quickly that His sandal nearly fell off his foot! He fled to her arms because he knew she would comfort Him, knew that she would always be with Him, would always help Him. We should know that we, too, can run to Mary — who offers us perpetual help — whenever we need to do so.

I would be surprised if there are many Catholics who can't easily conjure up a mental image of this picture. For many of us — myself included — it's the first icon we ever saw. A copy of Our Lady of Perpetual Help hung on the wall of my family's home in New Jersey for years. It seemed like she was watching over me as I was growing up, and I felt I could always turn to her whenever I needed help. I knew, without having to be told, that she offered a special kind of help, one that would never fail me and would never judge me harshly. I remember that as a boy I would stand before that picture, looking at the tender and protective way that Our Lady held the Christ Child in her arms. That tenderness seemed proof of her unfailing help. It made me believe that she would care for me in the same way.

I left New Jersey a long time ago, but I never parted company with Our Lady of Perpetual Help. On the day of my ordination more than fifty years ago, I was very pleased to know that there was a beautiful version of this icon hanging by one of the side altars in Sacred Heart Church in Yonkers, New York, the Capuchin church in which I was ordained. On what can be considered the most important day of my life, Our Lady of Perpetual Help was there, still watching over me, still offering me help and protection that would never fail, and I knew that whatever life might bring my way, her help would never falter.

When we think of Our Lady, which we should do often, we should never forget that she is ever available to us. Her help and her prayers are a constant in our lives. Even when we feel most alone she is leading us. Even when we walk the Way of the Cross, she walks with us. Her help, like the help of the entire Body of Christ, does not ebb and flow, like the tides; it is perpetual. And that is a fact for which we should be forever grateful.

Prayer

Holy Mother, dear Lady of Perpetual Help, we turn to you in times of trouble and need, but also in times of joy. Let us never lose confidence in your loving mercy for all your children, but rather give us the grace to draw all souls into the goodness of Christ through you. In the Name of Jesus Christ, Our Lord. Amen.

28
Jesus, Most Obedient

"Christ Jesus, who, though he was in the form of God, did not count equality with God a thing to be grasped, but he emptied himself, taking the form of a servant … he humbled himself, and became obedient unto death, even death on a cross. Therefore God has highly exalted him and bestowed on him the name which is above every name."

— Philippians 2:6-9

It seems a strange and paradoxical concept that the Second Person of the Blessed Trinity had to be obedient, doesn't it? Yet, His obedience to the Father became the source of all blessings for the human race. And this obedience was hardly a trifling matter for Him; it was obedience unto death. Think for a moment of the agony in the garden. His decision to suffer death for the sins of mankind caused Him to sweat blood in agony. It was a decision that required great resolve to carry through to the end, for it was a decision that would cost everything. To me, the ultimate test of obedience for Jesus was this: when He chose His Father's will in the face of extreme temptation to save himself.

In the movie *The Passion of the Christ*, we see the devil tempting Jesus in the Garden of Gethsemane. Surprisingly, the devil is dressed like a monk and speaks with a very soft, suggestive voice saying, "Isn't it too hard for one man to take on the sins of the whole world?" An ordinary man would have given up at that moment, but Jesus chose instead to "reject Satan and all his works and all his empty promises." To symbolize this, He then crushed the head of a serpent that crawls from beneath the devil's robes. It is a brilliant scene and illustrates the full weight of Jesus' decision.

We should never minimize the true self-renunciation and difficulty that obedience requires. At the same time, we should not exaggerate them but look at the magnificent blessings that flow from every act of authentic obedience. This last point is actually a lesson that I learned (and am still learning) from my own experience of religious obedience. I hope that the following story will show you what I mean.

Almost forty years ago, I was asked by the saintly Cardinal Terence Cooke, then-Archbishop of New York, to open a retreat house for priests in a very posh area north of New York City. Up to that point, I had been looking forward to spending my priesthood ministering to the inner-city poor. I was not at all happy about the cardinal's plan, which was so opposed to the plan I had developed for myself! In fact, I was devastated, but I agreed to his wishes, knowing in my heart that his will represented the will of God for me in this case.

In accepting this assignment I felt that I was surrendering all my hopes. Yet, the blessing that resulted from that small act of obedience has continued for four decades: some fifty priests who had left the priesthood came back to ministry through Trinity Retreat; hundreds of priests have lived there while making transitions in their lives, and literally thousands of good priests have had their priesthood fortified by retreats. What blessings have flowed from that one act of obedience to Cardinal Cooke — who, by the way, would have been very kind and understanding, if I had chosen to reject his request.

Jesus, the Son of God, is the most obedient of all men. Our small acts of obedience pale in comparison to His. His obedience overturned the consequences of the disobedience of Adam and Eve, bringing blessing in its place. All obedience involves some denial of self. His obedience, however, required far more. It required an overwhelming self-emptying. It required the One who is equal to the Father to "become like a servant."

So, Jesus really understands what obedience is. Because He does, He can meet us at those decision points in our lives when real obedience becomes difficult, when we would rather do something else, when we feel like slaves to others or empty of all that is legitimately ours. I urge you to reflect on your own particular call to holy obedience and turn to Him for help in doing the right thing, fully confident that superabundant blessings and true joy will flow from being obedient to the divine plan.

Prayer

O Jesus, Most Obedient, You are the model of obedience for all who struggle to do what is right in this world. Teach us obedience, not just as a matter of external conformity but as a way of life, and we will trust the guidance of Your Holy Spirit to lead us on the way to heaven. Amen.

29

Mary, Queen Conceived without Original Sin

> "The Most Holy Virgin is that blessed woman who was to crush with her heel the head of the infernal serpent. God, in creating Mary immaculate, scores His great victory over the devil; He reestablishes His sovereignty over the earth, God reenters creation as Master!"
>
> — Saint Peter Julian Eymard, Founder of the Congregation of the Blessed Sacrament

The dogma of the Immaculate Conception is one of the most difficult teachings of the Church to understand. Yet, it holds within it an essential truth about Mary and Jesus that deepens our devotion to both. Let me clarify something about this dogma that is often misunderstood — namely, that the term Immaculate Conception describes the conception of Mary, not that of Jesus. Mary was and is a member of the sinful human race, and so it took a special intervention of God at the moment of her conception in the womb of her mother, Saint Anne, to keep her free from any taint of original sin. This is the Immaculate Conception, a privilege that no other person in history could claim except Adam and Eve — before the Fall! When we talk about Mary being conceived without original sin, we should realize that we are saying something essential about Jesus, too. Since God was His Father, it was Mary who gave Jesus His humanity, His human nature, His biological reality. But because Mary was sinless from the moment of conception, it was impossible for Him to inherit the sin of Adam from her. It wasn't strictly *necessary* for Mary to be sinless in order to give birth to Jesus (in fact, the Protestants think she had sinned), but the Church teaches that it was fitting, appropriate, and perfect for her to have been a totally clean vessel in which Jesus, the Christ, could enter our world. That is the substance of the doctrine.

Let us dwell for a few moments on the power of Mary's sinlessness. Sinlessness — that is, purity — is a foreign concept to our modern culture, isn't it? We have a hard time getting our minds around the notion of a person who never experienced sin, never committed sin, and never even wanted to sin. Yet, Mary has a sort of mystical power over sin that bears great authority and can strengthen those who are weak or faltering in any area of faith or morality. We need her power and example as our guide in a very impure world.

First of all, purity has the effect of drawing people to all that is good, innocent, and holy. Mary's sinless life reminds us of the goodness of God in much the same way that a child reminds us of the beauty of innocence. Believe me, when you come from Jersey City and have lived in New York City for decades like I have, you need to be reminded of goodness and innocence as often as possible. Yet, in the long run, purity is more attractive than sin, and the human heart cannot stand a life of impurity for long. Even hardened criminals sometimes pay tribute to the value of purity (if in a strange way) when they tattoo images of Our Lady on their bodies. Such images remind them of better and purer times. Purity has that effect: it is powerfully attractive and always draws people to the good.

Purity also protects us from evil. Mary was, literally, untouchable by the Evil One in her lifetime because the devil is powerless without human cooperation, and Mary is the only human being beside Jesus who could not be seduced into sin. During the apparitions at Lourdes (1858) when Saint Bernadette was experiencing a vision of Our Lady, she heard a clamor of demonic voices coming from the nearby river yelling at Mary, "Begone! Begone!" In the midst of the clamor, the Immaculate Mary cast a sidelong glance in the direction of the voices, and Bernadette heard the demons run away screaming, following which peace was restored. What an astounding wonder of nature and grace is Mary's perfect purity. She needs no more than a glance to put demons to flight!

We call Mary the Queen Conceived without Original Sin because she was perfectly pure in her earthly life, and now exercises an immense power over baptized souls to keep us pure from the power of sin and evil. But, of course, she will never impose herself on us. We must place ourselves under the great authority of her purity and recommit ourselves daily to remaining free of sin. Mary will help us because it is her greatest joy to see us free from sin and full of grace. She wants to see us becoming more and more like her son every day.

Prayer

Dearest Mother of unsurpassable purity, pray that our hearts will be clean and pure and desire only what is of God. Teach us to reject all sin and evil, and transform the world through the power of sinlessness working in the hearts of Christians. We ask this in the Name of Jesus Christ our Lord. Amen.

30
Jesus, Most Patient

> "God is love, and he who abides in love abides in God and God in him."
>
> — 1 John 4:16b

As Catholics, we should not only take the above quotation from the First Letter of Saint John very seriously, we should rejoice in it, for these few words reveal to us something that neither science nor philosophy could ever discover. They reveal that the true nature of God — God's real essence — does not have to do with power. Instead it has to do with love. In these words we realize that God is very different from the myriad false gods and idols that human civilization has feverishly produced for millennia. They are idols of strength and domination, of control at the expense of others, of fiery judgment untempered by mercy. The real God — the God who is not the product of the human imagination — created us to be His beloved sons and daughters, not simply His servants, and certainly not His slaves.

This good news should enable us all to heave a big sigh of relief. Yet, it can be a strangely difficult truth to accept deeply into our hearts and souls. We are constantly aware of our own shortcomings, of all that "we have done and all that we have failed to do."[9] Our wrongdoings plague us so much that we often don't believe we are worth the infinite love of God, despite the fact that Jesus assures us that such love is eternally offered to us. As we confess the same sins for the umpteenth time, we are secretly sure that God must be losing patience with us (or perhaps has lost patience with us long ago). In this recognition of our own difficulty in rising above our sins, of transcending our humanity, we are in danger of doing what countless people before us have done. We are in danger of turning the God of love into a loveless God, of thinking that God must be like us: unable to forgive us, unable to forgive others.

Yet, Jesus shows us that God is endlessly patient. In parables such as that of the lost sheep (see Mt 18:12-14 and Lk 15:3-7), He of-

9 From the Penitential Rite.

fers us moving and poetic images of God's patient love for the least among us, for those who are lost — or believe they are lost. Reread this parable and meditate on it. Imagine Jesus as the Good Shepherd leaving His huge, obedient flock to trek into the hot, barren wilderness in search of the only sheep who did not follow Him. This single sheep makes little difference to the overall value of the flock, but it makes an enormous difference to the shepherd who loves each and every one of his sheep. In this simple story, Jesus shows us the depths of God's love, a love that is willing to risk everything to save those who believe themselves to be hopelessly lost, to save the one who thinks he has traveled beyond the love of God.

In early Protestantism, which came into being during the sixteenth century (although it had antecedents long before that), the idea of God's infinite patience for man was somehow eclipsed. In the rather somber theologies of Luther and Calvin, the stern, implacable judgment of God somehow seemed to replace — almost to devour — the love and patience of God. Yet, such an understanding of God is at odds with everything Jesus so patiently teaches us. As Catholics, we have always known that God's judgment is in some mysterious way a part of His love, and we have always known that Jesus is God's patience-with-man made flesh.

Jesus is the eternally patient One. He waits for us to turn to Him until after the last shred of hope is gone. This is one of the glories of our faith, that no matter what we have done Jesus will understand and forgive, if we but turn to Him. If you ever doubt the infinite patience of Christ, if you are ever tempted to exchange the loving God who is revealed in Jesus for a cruel god of human imagining, I urge you to meditate on a vision that Saint Faustina records in her diaries. She writes that at the moment of our earthly death Jesus comes to each of us. Picture that image in your mind. Imagine that as your soul is poised between life and death, between time and eternity, He is with you, not in judgment, but to plead with you to accept salvation. He comes once, and if He is rejected He comes again and then again. He patiently comes to each of us wanting but one thing — that we finally accept His love.

Prayer

Good Jesus, most patient with our sins and failings, look upon us with pity and help us to overcome the temptations of the world, the flesh, and the devil. As You have been so patient with us, help us also to be patient with the weaknesses of others, so that together we may finally enter the glories of heaven. We ask this in Your most holy and glorious Name. Amen.

31

Mary, Mother of the Church

"We believe that the Holy Mother of God, the new Eve, Mother of the Church, continues in heaven to exercise her maternal role on behalf of the members of Christ."

— *Catechism of the Catholic Church*, No. 975, quoting Pope Paul VI

While I have deep respect for the faith of my many Protestant friends, I have to say that their approach to Mary generally has a huge blind spot. They may admit that Mary had a special privilege in being called to bear the Messiah, and they may even admit that she is "blessed among women" (Lk 1:42) as the Gospel notes. But they are unable to see that Mary is more than just a simple disciple, that she was chosen from all eternity to have a continuous intercessory role in the life of all believers. Essentially, they under-appreciate the role of Mary as Mother of the Church, which is what Catholics know her to be.

Let's look at a few of the close associations between Mary and the Church. Mary was entrusted to the apostle John while she was standing at the foot of the Cross (see Jn 19:26-27). We know that Mary gave birth to Christ, but she also was present in the Upper Room on the day of Pentecost (see Acts 1:14), the very "birthday" of the Church, at the moment when the Holy Spirit came. Mary has been celebrated and venerated by "all generations" (Lk 1:48) of the Church. To her, we never fail to give honor and blessing. The Church is always very clear on this fundamental point: the Mother of Christ is the mother of all believers.

I am convinced that each Christian must discover for himself the truth that Mary is Mother of the Church. For some, it is easy, but for others, it is not immediately apparent and takes some tangible experience of her role on a wider level of the Church. While I have always had a strong belief in Mary's care for the Church, what solidified it for me was a most amazing story I once heard about Mary's personal preservation of the Faith among Japanese Catholics during two long centuries of persecution.

In 1854, Japan was opened to Western influences by Admiral Matthew Perry after being closed for more than two hundred years.

Soon after that, a French Catholic missionary went to Japan and built a small chapel in the outskirts of Nagasaki to evangelize the native population. It wasn't long before he had a number of curious Japanese watching him pray in the church and asking if they could see the Shrine to Mother Mary that he had built on the property. So he welcomed them and invited them to pray with him one afternoon. After their prayer, they began to ask him questions about his religion.

They first wanted to know if his religion had just one man who lived in Europe and was head over the whole Church. He nodded and said that was the Pope, and that seemed to make them very happy. Next, they asked him if the men who were leaders in the Church were married. He told them no, that the priests freely chose not to be married in order to serve the people better. When they heard that, they smiled with great joy. Finally, they asked if his religion honored the "Pure Lady in White," and he said that, of course, she was known as Mary, the Mother of Jesus. Upon hearing this, they were utterly ecstatic!

What joy it was for them to finally meet a true representative of the Faith that had been handed on to them from time immemorial. As it turned out, these Japanese Catholics were descendants of the *Urukami* people who had known martyrdom for their Catholic faith before Japan was closed to outside influences. They had kept the true faith without the benefit of clergy for over two hundred years! Amazingly, their "tests" for the authenticity of the Catholic faith were found in their three questions: fidelity to the Pope, clerical celibacy, and belief in the Immaculate Virgin Mary! It is hard not to see a truly miraculous occurrence in this event.

Truly, Mary preserves the Church's faith in a way that no one else can. She is the Mother of Christ before she is Mother of the Mystical Body of Christ, and her care, concern, and protection of the faithful is as diligent as the care she gave to Jesus in His earthly life. Perhaps we can pray for all other Christians who do not believe in Mary's essential role as mother of the faithful and Mother of the Church, so that they may not experience, shall we say, an awkward moment when they finally meet her face to face with us in the eternal Church of heaven!

Prayer

Blessed Mother of the Church and mother of every devoted follower of Jesus, fortify our faith in times of trouble, unite us more deeply to the Mystical Body of Christ, and bring to fruition within us all the blessings of heaven. We ask this through Jesus Christ our Lord. Amen.

32

Jesus, Light of Confessors

> 'We are the soldiers of peace, we are the army of the peacemakers, fighting for God and peace, *Deo et paci militantibus*. Persuasion, good example, loyalty to God are the only arms worthy of the children of the Gospel."
>
> —Sermon of Saint Bernard of Clairvaux preaching in defense of the Jews

Now, without a doubt, I have to start by clarifying a common misunderstanding. In the terminology of the Church's tradition, the title confessor does not refer strictly to a priest who hears confessions, although that is one application of the term. A confessor is one who confesses (or professes) the Catholic faith in a public way. A confessor may be a pastor, teacher, missionary, or preacher, but a confessor is never a martyr. Clearly some of the confessors of the Church came close to martyrdom, but God did not grant them that specific grace. These are the men who have publicly defended and explained the Catholic faith in a heroic way. I believe when one very current and well-known example, Pope John Paul II, is canonized, he will find himself in the Church's gallery of confessors. There has been no one in our contemporary world who has so explained, clarified, and defended the Catholic faith from attacks and confusions as well and as consistently as he.

I would be hard-pressed to think of a category of saints that is more important for evangelization than this one. Perhaps the martyrs have a greater number of canonized saints — and their lives are certainly more dramatic — but the spread of the Faith throughout the world has come primarily through preaching and patient teaching, according to Saint Paul. That is the essence of the vocation of the confessor saint, who does not hide his light under a bushel basket, but holds it proudly aloft in the darkness of his time so that others may be guided by it. In fact, we often use images related to light to describe what confessors do. We say that they "enlighten" our minds, "inflame" our souls, and "illuminate" our paths to the truth. The confessors are bold believers who confront heresies, rebuke sinners, refute errors, and patiently explain the mysteries of the Faith to all who will listen. I never cease to be inspired by these true heroes.

I am sure that the names of some of the greatest confessors are familiar to you. Virtually every founder of a religious order, unless he or she died a martyr, is considered a confessor. Saint Francis, Saint Dominic, Saint Benedict, Saint Alphonsus Liguori, Saint Ignatius Loyola are all in the ranks of confessors. Some of the greatest champions of the Faith are familiar names to us. The list of these great people in the life of the Church stretches back through all ages and cultures: Saint Augustine (North African), Saint Thomas Aquinas (Italian), Saint Francis de Sales (French), Blessed John Henry Cardinal Newman (English), Saint Columba and Saint Patrick (Irish), Saint Martin de Porres (Peruvian/African), Saint Charbel (Lebanese), Saint Damian of Molokai (Belgian), and the list goes on. Padre Pio, too, was officially canonized a confessor.

As a priest and a preacher, I can appreciate the very grave need for confessors of the Faith in every day and age. God does not hesitate to raise up some of the best of each generation and endow them with great gifts for spreading the Faith. However, not one of these individuals would ever claim that his gift for the work belongs to himself. Whether it be natural talent, intelligence, dynamic personality, or just plain charisma to change hearts, the confessor knows that everything has come from the Light of Confessors, Jesus Christ. There is no other source of light for the mission.

We are all confessors in some way, are we not? Whether we hand on the Catholic faith to our children, teach catechism, witness to others from our life's experience, or actually preach the Gospel in public, Christ is the light of our confession of faith! And because they have a very hard job, let us never forget to pray for priests and bishops whose vocation is to bear public witness to the Faith. With the shadows of moral confusion deepening in the modern age, more than ever we will really need the Light of Confessors to help keep the world from falling into the darkness of sin and error.

Prayer

Lord Jesus Christ, You are the Light of the World and the eternal Light of Confessors, enlightening Your Church in every generation to spread the Catholic faith. Give us the strength we need to bear witness to the truth and bring Your Light to countless souls for the glory of God who lives with You and the Holy Spirit, now and forever. Amen.

33
MARY, QUEEN OF FAMILIES

> "Authentic devotion to Mary ... constitutes a special instrument for nourishing loving communion in the family and for developing conjugal and family spirituality. For she who is the Mother of Christ and of the Church is in a special way, the Mother of Christian families, of domestic Churches."
>
> — Blessed John Paul II, apostolic exhortation, *Familiaris Consortio*

The Marian title Queen of Families was inserted into the Litany of Loreto in 1995 by Pope John Paul II. Many have called him the "Pope of the Family" due to the immense impact that he had in strengthening the Church's teaching on the critical issues of human life, marriage, and the family.

Perhaps the whole of the Church's teaching about marriage and family can be summed up in this title, "Queen of Families." If we reflect a few moments on Mary's vocation, we will see that she is never detached from family. She said "yes" to the angel Gabriel in consenting to be the mother of the Messiah; she and Joseph both said "yes" to a marriage that would create the family in which our Lord would grow and develop; and together they said "yes" to many sacrificial commitments to parenthood which entailed the stigma of Mary being pregnant before her official marriage (see Mt 1:18-25), the traumatic midnight departure into Egypt (see Mt 2:13-15), their quiet family life in Nazareth (see Mt 2:23), and even Mary's final vigil with Jesus at the foot of the Cross (see Jn 19:25-27). Mary's calling was stamped with the emblem of fidelity to God's plan for her as wife and mother. That does not even take into account the larger vocation to spiritual motherhood that she exercises for the Church from heaven.

Mary understands the hardships of family life in the modern age. Even though her external circumstances were different, the dynamics of parenthood are remarkably similar in every age. Mary knew the stress of poverty and a harsh political environment. She was an immigrant, living in exile in Egypt, a foreign country. She also knew the drudgery of daily existence in keeping house and home together. She was familiar with the problems of pregnancy and family relationships, and the many challenges of being part of a small community. Mary certainly has the capacity to reign over our families as queen in the modern age — if we let her.

Mary also helps foster religious vocations in the family, if the parents pray for their children to know God's plan for their lives. My own parents must have prayed to Our Lady for my vocation because, while they never explicitly told me that they were doing so, it became very clear to me at a very early age that I was supposed to be a priest. I first recognized that I had such a vocation when I was seven years old and kneeling before a statue of our Blessed Mother. I am sure Our Lady had a very strong hand in getting me into the Capuchin order and later in directing me to be among the founding members of the Franciscan Friars of the Renewal, which celebrated its twenty-fifth anniversary as an order in 2012. We never could have pulled off such a thing on our own.

Mary is also a healer of families that are broken by division, pain, and suffering. She has a special care for families in trouble, and brings a unifying influence into families that are coming apart. I don't think that she could ever neglect a family that turned to her in their need, no matter how desperate. If we believe the famous motto "the family that prays together stays together," then certainly the family that invites Our Lady into their problems will experience some unifying effects by her presence. We have only to believe it and entrust ourselves to Mary on a regular basis, and the fruits of prayer will be evident.

I would finally note that Mary is the queen of the modern-day pro-life movement, which is really an effort to safeguard the sanctity of families as well as individual human lives. Mary helps to dissipate the fear of those facing difficult pregnancies or those who are trying to provide for their families under trying circumstances. Mary could be called the first pro-life warrior on the battlefield against the culture of death. She is the gracious lover of all God's precious children, born and unborn.

Today, let us take Mary into our homes in a very special way, enthrone her image in the heart of our families, consecrate our loved ones to her, and call on her in any need whatsoever. There is nothing that we can ask of the Mother of the Holy Family, the Queen of Families, that she will not grant us when we ask with tenderhearted devotion.

Prayer

> *Dearest Mother of the Holy Family and Blessed Mother of our own families, keep us strong and faithful in the face of the many challenges to family life in the modern age. Let us always feel your loving presence in the heart of our homes, and bind us more closely together in love. We ask this through Jesus Christ, Lord of our families forever and ever. Amen.*

34

Jesus, King of Patriarchs

> "Matthan [became] the father of Jacob, and Jacob the father of Joseph, the husband of Mary, of whom Jesus was born, who is called Christ. So all the generations from Abraham to David were fourteen generations, and from David to the deportation to Babylon fourteen generations, and from the deportation to Babylon to the Christ, fourteen generations."
>
> — Matthew 1:15-17

Patriarchy gets a bad rap in this age so dominated by feminist ideas, but the Church has always seen the biblical Patriarchs in the most positive of lights. They are our "fathers in faith," and the traditional list of the Patriarchs of the Old Testament is Abraham, Isaac, and Jacob. Joseph and Moses are sometimes included, as well. What powerful and interesting figures they were. The Letter to the Hebrews tells us, "These all died in faith, not having received what was promised but having seen it and greeted it from afar" (11:13). To call Jesus the King of all the Patriarchs, then, means something very transcendent. He is literally the fulfillment of all the desires of the people of faith represented by the Patriarchs. He is the long-awaited One who was also their son, in a human sense. More importantly, He is their Lord and King — and ours — because He reigns over the faith of us all.

In early 2012, I celebrated the sixtieth anniversary of my religious profession and was given a truly extraordinary gift by my good friend and colleague Father Eugene Fulton. It is perhaps the most meaningful gift of my whole life. Father Fulton commissioned an iconographer to create a beautiful Holy Family icon for me. This type of icon is painted on a large piece of wood with an exquisite image of the Madonna and Child in the center. On either side are smaller images of all the patron saints of my parents and siblings. It now hangs in a prominent place in Trinity Retreat House, and I have the joy of seeing it and praying before it every day. It reminds me of God's providence over my family and, by implication, over my whole ancestry on both sides of my family, dare I say all the way back to Adam.

Now, if you looked into my family tree you would find a good number of colorful characters, especially on my Irish side. You may not find too many saints. Most of my people were probably happy and possibly a bit surprised just to make it into purgatory — but you would certainly see that members of my family on both sides were faithful Catholics through many generations. And when I ask to whom we may attribute that fidelity, the answer is clear. The fidelity of a family to God down through the generations cannot be attributed to any one individual's strength or virtue, even though virtuous example is necessary for handing on the Faith. That kind of long-term fidelity can only be due to the grace of the One who stands outside of time looking down on our families with love. He who is God of Abraham, Isaac, and Jacob is also the One who blesses to the thousandth generation those who fear Him (see Ex 20:6).

Any person of faith has to recognize the severe challenges to family life we all face today. In fact, I would say that attacks on the family are one of the atrocious hallmarks of the twentieth and twenty-first centuries. Families have experienced the literal splintering of their family trees through divorce, which has been made casual and easy virtually everywhere in the world. Not only the legalization but the encouragement of contraception and abortion has had devastating effects on family size, to be sure, but also on the religious faith of those who engage in these terrible and terribly sad practices. Pornography and the pervasive moral relativism that permits it to permeate (what's left of) our culture have had deeply destructive effects on families, especially on our young people, who are so vulnerable to these negative influences.

In the face of all this modern warfare on families, we must never lose heart. We must trust in the King of Patriarchs, who reigns over families. Can it be that He who formed His original Chosen People out of the descendants of Abraham and Sarah — one family — is unconcerned about these attacks on family life? Nothing could be further from the truth. We have all experienced the fallout of our inhumane culture on our families. We cannot defeat it alone, but we can do what the Patriarchs did from the beginning: they confided their cares to God and trusted in His grace to save them, to keep their families together as they waited for God's grace to prevail in the world. Their fidelity was rewarded with a blessing, to the thousandth generation. Now, let us ask the King of Patriarchs for that same blessing. He is only too happy to give it!

Prayer

King of Patriarchs and Lord of our faith, we turn to You in our desperate need to keep our families in Your grace in an age which militates against the sanctity of family life. Grant us Your abundant blessing, now and always, and keep us faithful to Your Church through all generations. We ask this in Your most holy and glorious Name. Amen.

35
Mary, Queen of Peace

> "Do not ever be troubled, do not ever be afraid, you have nothing to fear. Isn't the Immaculate perhaps aware of everything? If this were not true, we would be in great trouble indeed. No one can hurt us without God's permission, or even without the Immaculate's permission. Therefore, everything is in her maternal hands. … Let us just allow her to lead us ahead every day, every minute a little more."
>
> — Saint Maximilian Kolbe

In my years of experience with people of all walks of life and all cultures, whenever I would ask parents what they wanted for their children, they would invariably give me the exact same answer: "I just want my child to be happy." Parents just want the best for their children, in this life first, and then, even if they have never really thought about it, in the life of heaven, too (but, honestly, that is usually an afterthought!). There is an innate desire for their children to find happiness, however they define it. The Blessed Mother's desire for her children is exactly the same. She only wants our happiness, defined in spiritual terms as peace. That is why we call her the Queen of Peace.

Now, peace has both an external and an internal dimension. It is true that society tends to define peace simply as an absence of war, but the effect of that kind of peace is not to be downplayed. Society needs peace for its proper functioning and survival. Peace is a necessary precondition for human happiness, even in a worldly sense. Because of that, Our Lord attaches a blessing to those who make it their aim to pursue peace in a troubled world: "Blessed are the peacemakers, for they shall be called sons of God" (Mt 5:9).

Just after she won the Nobel Peace Prize, Mother Teresa served as a peacemaker in war-torn Lebanon. In the midst of the Arab-Israeli conflict in 1982, Mother Teresa announced that she would go without protection to Beirut to rescue fifty orphans and handicapped people who were trapped in a hospital with very little food. Against all military advice, she found someone who would drive her and her sisters into the war zone, and a cease-fire was declared for several hours while the Missionaries of Charity and other helpers rescued the vulnerable people. A story was told of her taking a baby into her arms who had been crying inconsolably for hours. As soon as the baby felt the touch of Mother Teresa, she stopped crying and was able to be fed.

This story illustrates, I think, the power that a consecrated person such as Mother Teresa can have in a war, not only war among nations, but also in the heart of a small child. Having known Mother Teresa well, I am convinced that no one was more devoted to Mary than she was. It was through her deep Marian spirituality that she invited the Queen of Peace into that place of war with very tangible effects. Soon after she conducted her rescue mission a permanent cease-fire was declared, and the ever-fragile Middle East peace was once again restored. My point is that there is really no limit to the power of Mary's peace. All she needs is to be invited into situations of conflict, and there the Queen of Peace does her work.

Mary's peace reigns where men and women of faith bring that peace to others. How often have I seen people take up the Rosary in times of turmoil and find that there is some tangible lessening of the power of evil or strengthening of heart needed to get through the problems confronting them. Mary's peace doesn't promise to take away conflict in all circumstances. She cannot and does not nullify the effects of human sinfulness. However, her mere presence brings an aura of peace to every war, whether in the heart of a person or in society, and her peace will prevail if we let it.

What conflicts in our lives need Mary's peaceful presence today? Into whose lives can we invite the Queen of Peace to reign and establish peace once again? How often have we taken seriously the power of the Rosary to wipe out the power of sin and chaos? The Queen of Peace waits for her invitation to enter our conflicts. She is waiting to bring us the peace of her son, a peace "which passes all understanding" (Phil 4:7).

Prayer

Holy Mary, gentle Queen of Peace, graciously bring God's gift of peace to the conflicts of our lives and world, and reign over us with your mercy. May your consoling presence transform us into instruments of peace in our world and bestow upon us the blessings of the world that never ends. We ask this through Christ our Lord. Amen.

36

Jesus, Master of Apostles

"For you, Eternal Shepherd, do not desert your flock, but
through the blessed Apostles
watch over it and protect it always, so that it may be governed by those
you have appointed shepherds to lead it in the name of
your Son."

— Preface I of the Apostles, *Roman Missal*

I wrote a few pages ago about the role of confessors in bearing public witness to the Faith. That is essential for the livelihood of the Catholic faith in the world. Here, however, I want to speak about something even more fundamental — namely, the Church itself, that makes public witness to the Faith possible. This Church — which, in the Creed, we call "one, holy, catholic, and apostolic" — is based on a solid foundation of apostleship. This is how Christ, Master of the Apostles, set it up. Let me use an image to explain this.

When I was growing up I noticed someone building a house in my neighborhood, and I distinctly remember asking my dad why the workers were always busy but, for a long time, no walls were going up. He told me that about thirty percent of the work on any house or building has to be done underground before the workers can even begin to put up any walls. What a fascinating concept that was for me as a young boy. But it all made sense, because without the moorings underground, the structure would topple with the first serious storm. It was my introduction to the idea of the importance of a foundation, and it taught me a few good lessons about the Church, too.

This was Church Lesson Number One: The Twelve Apostles are the actual foundation of the Church, according to the will of Jesus. Each of the Gospels contains the list of names of the twelve men He personally chose to be the foundation for the spiritual structure of the Church through all subsequent ages. With Saint Peter as the living symbol of that foundation, He said: "You are Peter, and on this rock I will build my church, and the powers of death shall not prevail against it" (Mt 16:18). In other words, when describing the only structure He ever built for himself, the Lord used the image of an unmoving, solid substance — rock — to indicate how firmly it had been placed in history for its mission of transmitting the Catholic faith to generation after generation. He wanted there to be no doubt in anyone's mind that His Church would remain immovable through all the storms of time.

Church Lesson Number Two is equally important: The bishops are the successors of the apostles throughout history. It is easy and perhaps somewhat tempting to get into the business of criticizing bishops for not leading the Church as we think they should. Let me tell you, there may be plenty of material for commentary, especially in these precarious times, but perfection is not part of the bishop's job description. Bishops have a tough job, and I would venture to say that the vast majority of our bishops are good and holy men who are doing their best to keep their dioceses founded on the Rock of Peter. Let us not be too quick to criticize these men who have the Twelve as their spiritual ancestors.

Church Lesson Number Three is my favorite: Despite even the colossal failures of Church leaders, the Church will endure to the end of time, precisely because of the grace of Christ. I love the humorous story that was once told about Napoleon who bragged to an Italian cardinal that he could destroy the Church without much trouble if he wanted to. The cardinal responded somewhat dryly: "If eighteen centuries of bishops have not been able to destroy the Church, I daresay you won't have much luck." Such is our faith in the apostolic foundation of the Church and the trust we have in the Holy Spirit's guidance through the ages. Jesus has promised to be with His Church until the end of time (see Mt 28:20). That promise is fulfilled in the guidance of our clergy in every day and age.

Now, as for real living bishops and priests, there is nothing better we can do for the Church than to pray for them — and I mean on a daily basis. I am convinced that we don't help them spiritually enough, but if we really believe in the Church, we will pray for these successors of the apostles as diligently as we pray for our own families. This may be Church Lesson Number Four: The Church's spiritual-foundation stones are strengthened by our prayers. Without them, our Church would begin to crumble.

Prayer

O Lord and Master of the Apostles, give us always a profound spirit of gratitude for Your Church and Your Apostles who are its foundation both in time and eternity. Keep us always united with them and bless them in their mission of keeping the Faith alive through all the ages. We make this prayer in Your most holy Name. Amen.

37

Mary, Queen of the Most Holy Rosary

"The Rosary is my favorite prayer. A marvelous prayer! Marvelous in its simplicity and its depth."

— Blessed John Paul II, October 29, 1978

Catholics rightly call Mary the Queen of the Most Holy Rosary because the power of the Rosary manifests Mary's great love and protection for all her children. Never will we be disappointed in asking anything from Mary through the recitation of the Rosary. Our queen wishes to draw us closer to Christ through this magnificent devotion, but I am convinced that we just don't pray it enough or with enough devotion. What miracles would happen if we did!

It is hard to overestimate the spiritual power of the Rosary, which has been a staple of Catholic devotion since at least the eleventh century. The faithful have seen numerous miracles spring from this humble string of beads. Thanks to the influence of my family and the wonderful sisters who taught me in school, I have prayed the Rosary from my youth with great fruitfulness. When I entered the Capuchins at the age of seventeen, I simply took it for granted that the Rosary would be part of my daily life, and so it was.

While it is difficult to pinpoint the exact origin of the Rosary devotion, its great popularity came primarily at the hands of Saint Dominic, the founder of the Dominicans, in the thirteenth century. Saint Dominic was alarmed about a particular heresy of his day that taught that the material world was evil and that the power of the devil was equal to the power of God. Well, a strong saint like Dominic was not going to sit around and let heretical preachers win the day at the cost of souls. So, he began what we might call today a Rosary Crusade all throughout Europe. Through it, he converted many souls back to the true faith.

Traditionally, the Rosary consisted of one hundred fifty beads representing in a symbolic way the one hundred fifty psalms of the Old Testament. As we know, these beads are divided into twenty decades of mysteries in which the faithful meditate on the joyful, luminous, sorrowful, and glorious moments of the lives of Jesus and Mary. Blessed John Paul II, in his encyclical *Rosarium Virginis Mariae* (2002), calls the Rosary a "school of Mary," and "a compendium of the Gospel" in which the faithful are "led to contemplate the beauty on the face of Christ and to experience the depths of his love." How beautiful and how true! The Rosary has been a source of profound conversions to the faith, the correction of morals, and the growth in holiness of countless souls. What most people don't know, however, is that it is also a real protection from disaster and evil.

Perhaps the most miraculous story I have ever heard of the Rosary came out of the terrible event of the atomic bombing of Japan at the end of the Second World War. In a rectory just eight blocks from the center of Hiroshima, on August 6, 1945, eight Jesuit priests were engrossed in praying the Rosary at the very moment of the bomb's impact. They survived the explosion unscathed. A half million people died in the bombing, but none of the Jesuits had lasting injuries from the explosion or negative effects from the radiation. All lived a normal life span. Can we attribute this to mere luck? The same thing happened to Saint Maximilian Kolbe's Franciscan community in Japan when a second atomic bomb was dropped on the city of Nagasaki just days later. The Garden of Mary Immaculate, which is what Saint Maximilian called his friary, was untouched by the explosion. Those Franciscans prayed the Rosary daily. Again, we must ask if such an event can be attributed to luck alone.

It cannot be emphasized enough that the seemingly repetitive prayer of the Rosary is not just rote prayer; it is meant to be a contemplation of the mysteries of the life of Christ from the point of view of His mother. Those who pray the Rosary regularly, and with true devotion, know that a real peace comes into the lives of those who are devoted to Mary, Queen of the Rosary. She never disappoints those who turn to her in this most beautiful of Marian devotions. Perhaps, today, she is inviting you to "contemplate the Face of Jesus" with her in the mysteries of the Rosary. If you accept the invitation of the Queen of the Holy Rosary, don't be surprised if your life changes forever.

Prayer

Dearest Mother and Queen of the Most Holy Rosary, fill our lives with a fervent spirit of prayer and meditation upon the holy life of our Lord Jesus. As you were privileged to nurture Him during His life on earth, so help us to know Him more profoundly by the contemplation of His mysteries, who lives and reigns with the Father and Holy Spirit, now and forever. Amen.

38

JESUS, TEACHER OF THE EVANGELISTS

> "The Church has always and everywhere held and continues to hold that the four Gospels are of apostolic origin. For what the apostles preached in fulfillment of the commission of Christ, afterwards they themselves and apostolic men, under the inspiration of the divine Spirit, handed on to us in writing: the foundation of faith, namely, the fourfold Gospel, according to Matthew, Mark, Luke and John."
>
> — Second Vatican Council, *Dei Verbum*

Many of the particular categories of saints we are addressing in this work (apostles, martyrs, confessors, etc.) have both a literal meaning and a spiritual meaning. The apostles, for example, are literally the twelve men chosen by Christ, but the term can figuratively designate any person who carries out an apostolate for the salvation of souls. The same is true for the category of saints we are now considering, the Evangelists. There are only four actual Evangelists, the writers of the Gospels — Matthew, Mark, Luke, and John — but there are many "evangelizers" in a spiritual sense. When we speak of Jesus Christ as the Teacher of the Evangelists, we are speaking directly of the One who inspired those four men to put His Gospel message down on paper for future generations, but we are also speaking of Him who is the Message itself which the Church preaches throughout the centuries.

When I think of some of the great evangelizers I have known over the years, I am always very aware that Jesus works as much today in His Church as He did at the very day of Pentecost. A non-Catholic friend of mine was visiting me one day as I watched a program on EWTN featuring the great Catholic preacher Archbishop Fulton J. Sheen. My friend, who knew nothing of Bishop Sheen, listened for a minute and then exclaimed, "Wow, this man is charismatic! Be careful, he just might make me Catholic!" Apparently, my years of working on the guy's faith had less impact on him than one minute's worth of Bishop Sheen's preaching! But that really is the point about communicating faith, isn't it? We need holy teachers in every age to strengthen and confirm our faith, to expand it and deepen it so that we ourselves may become holy.

I don't think there is a greater evangelist in the modern age than Mother Angelica. I distinctly remember the day she called me on the phone to ask me to do a show on her network. Well, actually, Mother didn't really ask me to do it, she *told* me I was going to do it. That "invitation" to teach the faith to millions has lasted for many years now, and no one has benefited more from it than I. Over the years, Mother has recruited, literally, hundreds of the Church's best teachers to broadcast the living Catholic faith to more than one hundred fifty million homes worldwide. What an astounding feat! By the way, she founded EWTN for the salvation of souls the same year that the utterly iniquitous MTV was founded, seemingly for the destruction of souls. This is just another example of God's good timing.

In our age, so heavily influenced by television and the mass media, we can easily forget the primary lesson of the four Evangelists: While preaching is a necessary means of bringing people to salvation, the Faith communicated in written form has a lasting impact on the world because it endures for many generations. The four Gospels and the other books of the New Testament are certainly the most splendid example of that truth, but following them, the Church has amassed for our spiritual benefit a treasury of writings that is extraordinarily impressive: the letters of great saints like Ignatius of Antioch, accounts of martyrdom and holiness, the sermons and reflections of the Fathers of the Church, great spiritual classics like the *Imitation of Christ*, as well as the voluminous writings of the great Doctors of the Church. Even the erudite and (if you ask me) sometimes rather boring encyclicals and writings of popes are part of that effort to leave a written record of truth for posterity. Christ is the Teacher of the Evangelists in every age. He is the source of their wisdom, zeal, and creativity in leading souls to heaven.

Perhaps this would be a good time to ask ourselves what our own contribution has been to the effort of saving souls. Have we ever given a pamphlet to someone else to help that person come to faith or to the Church? Have we actually sat down and taught the Catholic faith to our children or grandchildren, or given them resources to strengthen them in their personal journeys to God? I can tell you that while you may not see the fruit of your labors in this life, Jesus, Teacher of Evangelists, does indeed bless every effort we make to evangelize and bring others home to Him.

Prayer

> *Blessed Lord and Teacher of the Evangelists, pour forth the abundance of Your truth upon our souls and upon all who seek eternal salvation. Fill us with the wisdom of the evangelists and teachers around us so that we can pass through this vale of tears and reach the life of heaven. We ask this in Your most holy Name. Amen.*

39

Mary, Comforter of the Afflicted

"In dangers, in doubts, in difficulties, think of Mary; call upon Mary. Let not her name depart from your lips; never suffer it to leave your heart.... While she holds your hand, you cannot fail."

— Saint Bernard of Clairvaux

A mother can and should be an endless source of blessings for her children, and among the greatest of these maternal blessings is the ability to comfort in times of trouble and pain. Mary is rightly seen as the preeminent model of a mother consoling her children. Thus the Church is right to assign her the title of Comforter of the Afflicted. Before I explain further I want to mention that I cannot remember even a single instance in which I have turned to Mary in need or affliction when I have not been comforted in some very concrete and very real way. In my many decades as a Franciscan and as a preacher, I have always directed people to run to her without hesitation in times of trouble and sorrow. I have full confidence that no one has ever been turned away empty-handed. To this day, I bring not only my own needs but the needs of many other afflicted children to Mary, needs of those who otherwise would not have the consolation they require to withstand the sorrows of life.

Mary is shown in the Gospels as standing at the foot of the Cross, comforting her son in His time of greatest need. Imagine that scene for a moment, if you will, and then recall that she is nowhere to be seen during His triumphal entry into Jerusalem the week before. Nor was she at the Last Supper. Neither was she to be found in the Garden of Gethsemane, where an angel was sent by the Father to console Jesus. Rather, she is present as an almost solitary figure at the point when virtually everyone else had abandoned Him. She is powerless to stop the unjust killing of her beloved son, and she knows this. She comes to Calvary not to alter what she knew by faith to be the will of God. She comes in solidarity with the suffering Christ and out of deep motherly love. She knows her powers are limited, but she does all she can to provide Him with the last bit of earthly consolation that He will have. At that central moment of salvation history she is the Comforter of the Afflicted Christ.

Let us imagine further. On the next day, Holy Saturday, before Jesus is resurrected, and while the disciples are cowering in the Upper Room for fear of retaliation, she is there with them, too, strengthening them in their loneliness, grief, and affliction. The Gospels give us the impression that she remained with them throughout the whole fifty-day period after Christ's resurrection, up to the day of Pentecost. Even at that point, the Acts of the Apostles tell us that she is still with them, strengthening them to receive the Holy Spirit, which she knew they would need to face the persecutions and martyrdoms that would follow. What Mary was to Jesus at Calvary, she continued to be in Jerusalem for the early Church. She has remained that for all generations of Christians to follow: she is the Comforter of the Afflicted.

The unceasing testimony of Christians throughout the centuries bears witness that Mary exercises this most vital function of consolation and comfort for all who belong to her son. We must never hesitate to turn to her in times of sorrow and distress — whatever the origin of our troubles. When a mother sees the suffering of a child she does not ask why the child cries or whether the reason is just or unjust. She only seeks to alleviate the sorrow and to help the child derive some true benefit from it. She is our mother, and we are her children. Mary *wants* to be included in all of our most trying moments. She has innumerable healing graces to bestow upon us if we will but turn to her and ask her to help us. In the apparitions of the Miraculous Medal, Saint Catherine Labouré saw Our Lady as wearing jewels on her fingers, most of which shone with light. She asked Our Lady why some of the jewels were not radiant while many other jewels were. Mary replied that the jewels that did not give off light represented all the graces that the faithful did not ask for but which she so wished to provide for them. Take that to heart; it is a great lesson for us all.

We are all aware that our time on this earth is full of sorrows and afflictions, but how often do we go to Mary, as Saint Bernard says, "in dangers, in doubts, in difficulties"? When we admit that we cannot handle all the challenges of life on our own, that is the moment when we find an avenue to address our problems. We need only turn to Our Lady, Comforter of the Afflicted, to receive help in all our afflictions. Like the most loving of mothers, Mary will run to our aid.

Prayer

Holy Mother, tender Comforter of the Afflicted, stand by us in all our sorrows and sufferings, just as you stood by the Cross of Jesus. Unite our afflictions to His, and bring us through them to the everlasting joys of heaven. We ask this through Christ our Lord. Amen.

40

Jesus, Strength of Martyrs

"O Lord Jesus, King of Martyrs, to those who must suffer torment and violence, hunger and fatigue, be Thou the invincible strength sustaining them in their trials and assuring them of the rewards pledged by Thee to those who persevere unto the end."

— Pope Pius XII, "Prayer for the Church of Silence," July 16, 1957

The heroism of martyrs in the face of evil is but a small window into their lives, a snapshot that we see after they died glorious deaths. It is never the whole story of their passion. We may think that they neither feared death nor caonsidered running away from their fate. The truth of the matter is that the martyrs were a lot like you and me. They were men and women of flesh and blood who could not have endured their agonizing deaths without another Strength to get them through the horror of death into the life of heaven. The deep inner beauty of the martyrs' stories is not so much in the shedding of their blood; it is in how they managed their moments of doubt and persevered in their fidelity to God to the end.

Jesus is sometimes called King of Martyrs because His martyrdom is the model for all others. In the Garden of Gethsemane, He agonized over the sins of the world and even begged the Father to take away the cup of His suffering. He felt all the weakness of human flesh, but He never abandoned His mission. His decision to do the Father's will was no less pure when He was standing before Pilate, betrayed by His own, mocked and scourged by the soldiers. He was also the model for martyrs as he walked the Way of the Cross. If we read any of the Passion narratives of the Gospels very carefully, we will see that at every moment of His agony He was saying "yes." This "yes" continued right up to the moment when, with His final breath, He cried, "Father, into thy hands I commit my spirit" (Lk 23:46). His heroism certainly came in the glory of His death. Yet, I see even more heroism in His continuous decision to accept death for our sake.

If we go back again to the stories of some of the most inspiring martyrs, we see that their heroic deaths are just the culmination of heroic lives dedicated to doing God's will.

One of my favorites among the martyrs is Saint Joan of Arc who, at the age of seventeen, was made the commander-in-chief of the armies of France. This girl led men into the thick of combat as if she were General George S. Patton, and she never lost a battle. When she was unjustly condemned and burned at the stake, she asked only for someone to hold up a crucifix before her eyes, so that Jesus, the Strength of Martyrs, would be the last image she would see in this world.

Saint Thomas More was the first of hundreds of astounding English martyrs whose deaths were among the cruelest of any martyrs in history. He had his head chopped off because he would not submit to King Henry VIII's plan to control the Church. When More ascended the platform he said, "I die the king's good servant but God's first." He had his kings in proper order.

Both Saint Perpetua and Saint Felicity, two early Roman martyrs, were young mothers in their early twenties when they were condemned to die in the arena for being Christians. Saint Felicity was pregnant, and her execution was delayed until she had given birth to her baby! Saint Perpetua had to endure multiple heart-wrenching pleas from her father who begged her not to "abandon" her children and family for the sake of what he thought was a meaningless death. Yet she saw her death as being far from meaningless. Eighteen centuries later we still tell the story of the fidelity to God of these two young women. In fact, their names are forever enshrined in the First Eucharistic Prayer.

It is impossible to know the number of those who have suffered martyrdom for the Christian faith, but I can tell you that there are many more martyrs than those who have been canonized. The list of martyrs is undoubtedly the Church's greatest badge of honor. How is it possible for mere human beings to remain faithful in the face of violent death? Only Christ, the Strength of Martyrs, makes such heroic sacrifice possible.

If we cling to Him in all times of stress or pain, call to Him in times of temptation, beg Him for the grace to remain faithful in all our duties and practices of the faith, He will give us His strength to undergo our own personal martyrdoms. It is unlikely that we will have to die for the Catholic faith, but if we do, the Strength of Martyrs will be with us. Christ himself will stand beside us.

Prayer

O Holy Lord Jesus, King and Strength of Martyrs, fill us with Your Spirit of sacrifice, and make us one with You in all the sufferings we have to endure, both in our daily duties and in our fidelity to the Catholic faith. Give us the grace to support all those who suffer, and teach us to look to Your cross as our only hope. We ask this in Your most holy Name. Amen.

41
Mary, Seat of Wisdom

"Mary is the secret magnet. Wherever she is, she draws Eternal Wisdom so powerfully that He cannot resist. Of all the means to possess Jesus Christ, Mary is the surest, the easiest, the shortest way, and the holiest."

— Saint Louis Marie de Montfort, from *True Devotion to the Blessed Virgin Mary*

This beautiful title of Mary, Seat of Wisdom, has been depicted in art for centuries, and particularly in artwork for educational settings. In these images, Our Lady is often shown as seated on a throne and holding the Child Jesus — Wisdom himself — in her lap. The Child Jesus is facing outward as if to display or offer Him to the world. She may be depicted standing and holding the Child Jesus in her arms, their heads tenderly touching. The implied message in the image is that she is both contemplating Him and giving Him to others. In such images, Our Lady is literally the repository of God's Eternal Wisdom for the world.

Now, living in what we like to call the "information age," we must be very careful not to fall into the trap of thinking that knowledge or information is actually wisdom. Knowledge is important for conducting human affairs — it even helps us to know about God — but it does not give us a relationship with God, nor does it teach us to do His will. That is the function of wisdom, which involves the heart more than the mind and must be achieved through reflection and prayer on God's actions in the world. Wisdom comes as the fruit of an interior attitude of silence and reflection and is definitely not the result of any quick-fix program. It is said twice of Mary in the Gospel of Luke that Mary "kept" or "reflected on these things in her heart" (2:19,51). This attitude of Mary's heart was noted in Scripture just before the Holy Family settled in Nazareth, where she had ample time to reflect on God and His works.

We have already contemplated the wedding feast at Cana in this little book. We shall do so for a moment again, because I think this event shows the effects of Mary's thirty years in the presence of Wisdom himself. In the dialogue between Mary and Jesus as recorded in the Gospel of John, we see that she had a deeply intuitive grasp of the divine plan. When she informed Jesus that the wine had run out, she was indicating that something momentous was to take place. She did not demand or beg Him to work a miracle, because true wisdom is humble and demands nothing of God. Rather, at that critical point she simply presented to Him the needs of others, renouncing her own attachment to Him from that moment on, and human history has never been the same. "Do whatever He tells you" (Jn 2:5) is the greatest wisdom statement ever uttered to mankind and also the last words we hear from Mary in the Bible. How fitting.

All those who exhibit true wisdom in their lives acquire that wisdom through the same Marian pattern of reflection on the mystery of Jesus. Formal education is for the privileged, but wisdom is for all, even the illiterate. One of my favorite saints, Saint Bernadette of Lourdes, was a poor uneducated girl who did not know how to read or write. Believe it or not, she did not even know her correct age because she couldn't count; yet, she consistently confounded the wisdom of the world with her candor. When she was cross-examined after the apparitions in 1858, she told a skeptical public official that the Lady had asked her to pray for sinners. The man scoffed and asked, "And what exactly is a 'sinner'?" Bernadette replied directly, "Sinners are those who love sin!" *Touché,* as they say in French.

Yet wisdom is more than retorts in tight situations. The wisdom of the simple often pierces heaven with tremendous insight. When Bernadette was about to die, the chaplain asked her to offer her life as a sacrifice, but she responded that it was no sacrifice to leave this world where it was so difficult to belong to God. True wisdom is not of this world but helps us get through it to heaven. Imagine the millions of souls who have received the wisdom that Bernadette has offered in Lourdes for more than one hundred fifty years for the healing and strength of all.

Our Lady's wisdom was profound. It was a way of looking at reality, a way that came from her perpetual contemplation of the mysteries of God that were present before her eyes in the person of her son Jesus. She has given us that eternal wisdom for the benefit of our souls. If the stories of the saints indicate anything, it is that we don't gain wisdom by long hours of study. We gain it by sitting at the feet of Him who came from Mary to save the world.

Prayer

Mother of Christ and Seat of Wisdom, graciously bestow divine wisdom upon us so that we may constantly see our world with the eyes of faith. Let us be generous stewards of wisdom, sharing it with others. May wisdom help to draw many souls out of this world into the life of heaven. We ask this in the most holy Name of Jesus. Amen.

42

Jesus, Eternal Wisdom

> "Our Blessed Lord left the world without leaving any written message. His doctrine was himself. Ideal and History were identified in Him. The truth that all other ethical teachers proclaimed, and the light that they gave to the world was not *in* them, but *outside* them. Our Divine Lord, however, identified Divine Wisdom with himself. It was the first time in history that it was ever done, and it has never been done since."
>
> — Archbishop Fulton J. Sheen, from *Life of Christ*, 1977

I have worked for many decades in educational environments, and I can tell you that the concept of wisdom in the ivory towers of academia is often rather abstract. But it doesn't need to be. As Archbishop Sheen so beautifully points out, Wisdom is a Person, Jesus himself, and no other religious system comes close to having this fullness of truth, this infinite depth of wisdom. All the Old Testament passages that speak of wisdom point to Jesus as the fulfillment of the teaching of the prophets and sages of Israel.

When talking about wisdom, we have to be aware of the distinction that Saint Paul made between the wisdom of God and the "wisdom of this world." There is a fundamental difference. He said, "Let no one deceive himself. If anyone among you thinks that he is wise in this age, let him become a fool that he may become wise. For the wisdom of this world is folly with God" (1 Cor 3:18-19). We call Jesus the Eternal Wisdom of God because by becoming human He brought into the world a way of viewing reality from the vantage point of eternity. When we adopt this view of reality, we see that our lives and the world around us are filled with meaning — not meaning that our minds supply, but meaning we can prayerfully discover. This often puts us in conflict with the standard understanding of things, which finds our world devoid of value except the value that we choose to impose on it. In the world's view, meaning is something we decide and which we can change at will. Conflict between the two views of reality is inevitable. Saint Paul even says that the worldly view of things is "folly" and "rubbish" (see Phil 3:8) when compared to God's perspective. But how hard it is to make ourselves see things the way God sees them.

Eternal Wisdom, in this sense, is not knowledge one can glean from a book. It is, rather, a perspective on things, a way of seeing the dimension of depth which is inherent in everything. Wisdom is not intelligence; it is perception from a much higher viewpoint. Imagine going up in a helicopter over the intersection of several highways and radioing down to give directions to the driver of a car who can't see which road is the one that will take him to his destination. The mass of intersecting highways looks confusing from the ground view, but from the helicopter, hundreds of feet above, the direction is clear. That is a weak analogy for how important Divine Wisdom is for us mortals. Without that eternal perspective we would be lost in the maze of conflicting paths that the world offers us for fulfillment. We don't need fulfillment; we need salvation.

For me, the Gospel teaching that most "confounds the wise" and expresses the essence of our faith is the teaching to love one's enemy. When you get to this teaching of Jesus, all bets are off. It is the dividing line between those who accept the wisdom of Christ and those who can't get beyond the wisdom of this world. To my knowledge, Christianity is the only religion or philosophy in history that has ever taught this hard truth. It had to be revealed by Eternal Wisdom himself in order for us to know it, because it so militates against the way we are all inclined to think. I don't believe for a minute that this teaching is easy to practice. It can only be lived through a life of grace. Yet, this eternal truth of the Gospel is also the only thing that could literally transform the world if we let it.

Allow me to end with a prayer that is not my own but which I picked up from another priest's sermon somewhere in my career. I am told that it was found on a piece of paper near a dead woman and child when the Ravensbruck concentration camp was liberated at the end of World War II. I have no doubt that a magnificent soul, purified by suffering and full of Christ's Eternal Wisdom, wrote it for our benefit. Bring this gem with you on your journey through life and you will undoubtedly grow in wisdom and grace.

Prayer

O Lord, when I shall come with glory into Your Kingdom, do not remember only the men of good will; remember also the men of evil. May they be remembered not only for their acts of cruelty in this camp — the evil they have done to us prisoners — but balance against their cruelty the fruits we have reaped under the stress and in the pain: the comradeship, the courage, the greatness of heart, the humility and patience which have been born in us and have become part of our lives because we have suffered at their hands. May the memory of us not be a nightmare to them when they stand in judgment. May all that we have suffered be acceptable to You as a ransom for them. "Unless a grain of wheat falls to the ground and dies ... " Amen.

43

Mary, Help of Christians

> "And a great portent appeared in heaven, a woman clothed with the sun, with the moon under her feet, and on her head a crown of twelve stars."
>
> — Revelation 12:1

Imagine for a moment that it is the early 1570s. Imagine also that you are in Europe and that like most people of that time you cannot help but tremble with dread. The armies of the Ottoman Turks are advancing. They've made enormous inroads into the Balkans, establishing their sovereignty over one Christian country after another. They have already attacked the very gates of Vienna and were only barely repulsed. An Ottoman fleet of enormous — unbelievable — size is poised to attack. You are painfully aware that Christian Europe is in mortal danger, that it soon may be overrun.

And then you are asked to pray with an intensity you have never known. The call comes from Pope Pius V himself, who has rallied Christian armies from all over Europe to make one last-ditch effort to defend their lands, to offer their lives for their beloved faith and for you. Your first instinct is to pray to Saint Michael, for he is "our defender in battle." But the pope insists on prayers to Our Lady under the title of Mary, Help of Christians. And so when you and countless others pray, the image in your mind is not of a powerful archangel with enormous pinions and a fiery sword defending the Christian world. It is of a young woman tenderly holding an infant — the very picture of defenselessness, the perfect image of vulnerability.

The Ottoman Turks should have won. Yet, they were defeated against all odds; their impressive navy left a mass of wreckage. Western Europe, at least, was spared for the moment. It was a seeming miracle and was attributed to Mary, Help of Christians, to the young woman who cradled her child in her arms as warriors rushed into battle.

This is the stuff of myth. Yet, it is not myth, but history. Our Lady, Help of Christians, is a title that goes back at least to Saint John Chrysostom, one of the Fathers of the Church. Yet, it was barely known until that time in the sixteenth century when all seemed lost. At that moment, the world recalled what it needed to recall, that Our Lady is truly the help of all Christians, and with that knowledge they turned the course of history.

I have to admit that when I look at the world around me, I sometimes wonder if all seems lost again. Whether we want to admit it or not, we are under siege — maybe not literally this time, but at least metaphorically, and certainly psychologically. The Church and her beliefs are regularly belittled, mocked, and attacked on television and radio. Internet comments about Catholicism are often appallingly vicious and even obscene. The government sometimes seems to act as if religious freedom can be restricted and restructured at a whim regardless of the Constitution. Enemy armies may not be at our gates, but we live in difficult times, far more difficult than American Catholics are used to.

How are we to deal with this? Prayerfully, patiently, and with real determination, of course. We cannot ignore the situation, and we certainly cannot betray our faith by surrendering to the culture that surrounds us, a culture that seems bent on self-destruction and certainly self-degradation. I do think it is time for us to remember Mary, Help of Christians, once again.

I urge you to pray to Our Lady under this title. I urge you to meditate on the image of the defenseless mother and child until you can see the truth in it. It is a better symbol of the infinite power of God than anything that represents worldly power can be. The power of God cannot be found in the clashing of armies or the winning of elections, or the imposition of the ideas of one group upon another. The power of God is only revealed in gentleness, caring, and love, in the tender love of a mother for her child.

As the prayers of countless souls to Mary, Help of Christians, saved a beleaguered Christendom four and a half centuries ago, may our prayers to her today help to bring hope to our dark and broken world.

Prayer

Mother of mercy and Help of Christians, you who have so wondrously protected and strengthened Christians throughout the centuries to be victorious over the powers of evil, continue to provide us with the grace necessary to stand strong for Christ against the evils of our own day, and so win the victory that His love promises to the faithful. We ask this in the Name of Jesus our Lord. Amen.

44
Jesus, Crown of Saints

"I arise today
Through the strength of the love of cherubim,
In the obedience of angels,
In the service of archangels,
In the hope of resurrection to meet with reward,
In the prayers of patriarchs,
In the preaching of the apostles,
In the faith of confessors,
In the innocence of virgins,
In the deeds of righteous men."

— From Saint Patrick's Breastplate, ca. AD 377

The Church long ago created a list that it uses to define the categories of sanctity and explain the diversity of saints in the life of the Church. Saint Patrick's list expresses some of it. It starts with the holy angels, of course, and goes through the Old Testament "saints" such as patriarchs and prophets, then proceeds to the canonized saints of the Church such as apostles, martyrs, confessors, virgins, and holy men and women. The list of categories is very helpful because it inspires us to find our niche in the overall gallery of Christian virtue throughout the centuries. Think of it as a Catholic Hall of Fame with all our greatest heroes found somewhere on that short list. More importantly, if we take our spiritual life at all seriously, we should seek to find a place on that list! These are the models that God puts in the world for our inspiration.

New Testament writers often use the image of a crown to describe the beauty of sanctity. Saint Paul says that the people of Philippi are his "joy and crown" (Phil 4:1) and urges us to fight for the "imperishable wreath" (1 Cor 9:27) that awaits us in heaven. Peter speaks of a "crown of glory" (1 Pt 5:4) and James a "crown of life" (Jas 1:12) that will belong to the saints. This list can be multiplied with many other references, but you get the picture. In a human sense, crowns are the most wonderful ornaments that we can create to signal the status of a person. Those who wear them are always very important, very special people. How much more important are the saints.

If there is one healthy habit I have had since I was a boy, it is what I would call (for lack of a better term) saint-watching. Undoubtedly, my propensity to hone in on saints of every shape and size has given me a continuous enthusiasm for my faith all these years. It is something that has always caused me to strive for a greater holiness myself, as far away from that as I may be. I also discovered along the way that saints and their teachings, their examples, and their virtue, helped to shape my life as a priest and molded me into what God wanted me to be (although I've still got a long way to go on that one). I can honestly say that I consider these astonishing examples of goodness, both in heaven and on earth, as friends who have walked with me on my journey. They left their deep imprint of love on my soul.

I liken the saints to the different colors and bits of glass in a marvelous stained-glass window viewed from inside a dark cathedral. Each expression of living holiness is a brilliant dash of color in the total mosaic, blending into the gorgeous luminosity of the whole work of art. Each helps to form the full image that the window shows to the world. Without a doubt, all the saints would say that their own unique piece of glass, no matter how colorful, would be nothing without the illumination that shines from the outside to light up the window. That is true in an absolute sense, but let's also recognize that each saint's life and example serves to magnify the one light and image of Christ in the world. In this sense, the saints are all radiant prisms through which Jesus, the Crown of Saints, allows His grace to flow.

Now, imagine this: Jesus Christ does not just wear the most beautiful crown of all the saints; He *is* the Crown that all the saints wear, in the same way that we would call something "the crowning glory" of an effort. He is the highest holiness of angels, the utmost confessor of faith, the most glorious spouse of virgins, the supreme king of martyrs, and the absolute font of all the sanctity exhibited by every holy man, woman, or child who ever lived. In Christ we find an inexhaustible wellspring of holiness that He can share with others.

Now, do you think that Christ, the Crown of Saints would deny holiness to you if you asked? Inspired by Him and the illustrious examples of all the saints, let us seek holiness with all our might, and be assured that it will be granted in abundance to any who *really* want it.

and be assured that it will be granted in abundance to any who *really* want it.

Prayer

Heavenly Lord and crowning glory of all saints, graciously set upon our heads the crown of holiness that is reserved for those who love God with all their hearts, souls, mind, and strength. Teach us to serve our neighbors heroically in our state in life so that we may draw many souls to heaven through the example of holy lives. We ask this in Your most holy Name. Amen.

45

Mary, Mystical Rose

"What was the color of that Blossom bright?
White to begin with, immaculate white.
But what a wild flush on the flakes of it stood,
When the Rose ran in crimsoning down the Cross wood.
In the Gardens of God, in the daylight divine
I shall worship the Wounds with thee, Mother of mine."

—Gerard Manley Hopkins, S.J., 1898

We have in Mystical Rose an exceptionally beautiful and evocative image for our Blessed Mother. You might recall how often roses were associated with Our Lady. Think of the May crownings and the way, as children, we heaped roses around the Blessed Mother's statue. From a very early time, the Christian faithful made the rose the predominant symbol of the Virgin Mary because the rose is a natural and beautiful symbol of our deep love for another person. It is not hard to imagine how the Christian tradition chose the rose as a symbol of our love for Mary's person, her beauty, and the special place she occupies in the work of salvation. I offer this next thought with the greatest of respect for her dignity, but I truly imagine that in her physical features Mary must have been the most beautiful of all women, given that she was the most pure and most blessed woman ever to have been born. But it is not Mary's physical beauty that we praise, it is the overwhelming mystical — that is, spiritual — beauty that radiates from Our Lady that makes us venerate her as Mystical Rose.

Not surprisingly, the earliest writers of the Church found references to Mary in the many biblical images of the rose. They spiritualized these references to show that Mary's immense inner beauty was the spiritual equivalent of the fragrant rose, and that she was deserving of all our love. In modern times, that connection has not diminished either. If you have any familiarity with the history of Church-approved apparitions you will know that roses are connected very significantly to the Blessed Mother in virtually all of them. In the apparitions at La Salette, France (1846), for example, she appeared wearing a garland of roses around her neck and had roses on her feet. There were also rose on the Virgin's feet in the more famous apparitions at Lourdes in 1858. Those familiar with the apparitions of Our Lady of Guadalupe more than three centuries earlier will remember that roses were the miraculous sign that the humble Indian unknowingly brought to the bishop. Other approved apparitions such as Pontmain, Beauraing, and Banneaux all included roses in some way!

I believe that no one testified to the mystical beauty of Mary more eloquently than Saint Bernard of Clairvaux, who is reputed to be the author of the famous Memorare prayer to Mary. He wrote: "Eve was a thorn, wounding, bringing death to all; in Mary we see a rose, soothing everybody's hurts, giving the destiny of salvation back to all. Mary was a rose, white for maidenhood, red for love … white in her love of God, red in compassion for her neighbor."

Above all, Mary, the Mystical Rose, brings spiritual beauty and love into our lives in a way that no one but God can do. Maybe you have experienced, as I have, tears welling up in your eyes when you read the touching story of a mother's devotion to her suffering son, or of a father's sacrifice of his life to save a child, or any account of someone's inspirational or heroic action taken out of love for another. Those tears come from an experience of true spiritual beauty. That movement of the emotions, wrenching of the heart, raising of the spirit is, literally, the effect of Mary's mystical love for you even if you may not identify it as such in the moment. Mary shares that inspiration in the way a rose exudes its fragrance into its environment. She is God's Mother, one so awesomely beautiful, fragrant in her virtues, and blessed in her union with Christ that she can communicate that love intuitively and actually to all the souls saved by her son

Let us not hesitate to take our overwhelming number of petitions, fervent prayers, concerns, sorrows, agonies, praises, love, and expressions of gratitude to Mary, our Mystical Rose. We should ask her to present them to God in a fragrant spiritual bouquet as only she can. She, who is the most beautiful of all God's creatures, will win for us the things we seek. I am convinced that when God beholds the beauty He has created in Mary, He must immediately say "yes" to everything she asks!

Prayer

Holy Mother of our Lord Jesus Christ, Mystical Rose and font of eternal beauty, fill our lives with God's loveliness. As you experienced the depths of His divine love here on earth, so give us a share of that love in the life to come. We ask this in the Name of Jesus, our Lord. Amen.

46

Jesus, the Splendor of the Father and the Brightness of Eternal Life

"In him was life, and the life was the light of men.
The light shines in the darkness,
and the darkness has not overcome it."

— John 1:4-5

Life and light are two words that sound very much alike in English, and they have always been among the greatest symbols of God. In fact, they are so great that the reaction of the human soul to them is universal. Life and light are symbols for God in virtually all religions, all cultures. No healthy person truly yearns for darkness or death, and no culture can really choose darkness over light or death over life for very long. As Catholics we should see that the universal longing of humankind for life and light is really a longing for the One who has the power to conquer the darkness of sin in our lives, the One whose power reaches beyond our biological deaths, granting us eternal life. In the simplest of terms, our longing for light and life is actually a longing for Christ. He is the one true bearer of God's light and the giver of eternal life, and He is rightly called in the devotional life of the Church the Splendor of the Father — that is, the mysterious and majestic source of all life and goodness.

Despite our yearning for life, death is still powerful in our world. Rooted in the primordial rejection of God by our first parents — a rejection that we echo far too often in our own lives — the yearning for death is our demand to have power over God's gift of life, to become our own gods, our own masters of life and death. Such pride and arrogance do not give up their hold on us easily. We have only to look to our recent past to see the proof of this. A fascination with death was inherent in Nazism and communism, systems that utterly rejected God, enthroning the will of man as the arbiter of all things and causing unprecedented destruction. Every day we encounter an acceptance of death, even a preference for it in our world. Think of the abortion industry, the growing acceptance of euthanasia, of Hollywood's routine depiction of horrific violence and death as mere entertainment. All these things and many more demonstrate the power of death in our time.

In contrast to this, there remains the gift of life that comes to us in Christ Jesus! His resurrection put a definitive end to the dominion of death in this world. If we truly are in Christ, we will reject death and embrace life.

Saint John's Gospel tells us that Christ is "the light of the world," and Jesus promises that "he who follows me will not walk in darkness but will have the light of life" (Jn 8:12). What a wonderful promise! By contrast, death is always enshrouded in darkness, which Saint Thomas Aquinas calls "the double darkness of both sin and ignorance" of human nature and society. As we look around us, we see much darkness. We see the power of death in our world. Lies and distortions are commonplace; good is mistaken for evil; the death of some is considered a reasonable exchange for the convenience of others. We see that the power of death is too strong for our sinful and fragile human nature to overcome. No amount of education or exhortation alone can undo the moral confusion of our times. There is only One who can penetrate the deep darkness of modern culture, One who can touch human hearts immersed in darkness or despair — Jesus Christ. His light "shines in the darkness, and the darkness has not overcome it" (Jn 1:5).

He who is Light and Life is called the Splendor of the Father with good reason! He reveals the brilliant, overwhelming love of the heavenly Father for all His children, regardless of the evils we may have committed. When facing the truth of our own sins, deceptions, and errors — as we all must — it is consoling to know that these realities are not final. They do not irrevocably condemn us. In fact, they are the condition of receiving the Father's Light and Life that comes to us in Jesus. Let us have great confidence in Christ's ability to overcome our faults and failings with a love that is eternal. Let us heed His call to turn from death and darkness to life and light. Let us have the humility to accept joyfully the brightness of eternal life He yearns to bestow on all who ask Him for it.

Prayer

Light and Goodness of the Father, bringer of Life to the whole world, Jesus our Lord, we thank You for loving us into existence, and for shining Your radiance upon us so that we can walk through the darkness of this world to the life that never ends. Consecrate us in Your truth and fill us with the light and life You promise to all who love You. We ask this in Your most holy Name. Amen.

47

Mary, the Gate of Heaven

> "Maiden-Mother, bearing the Word of God, you are the
> gate of paradise;
> in bringing God into the world you have unlocked for us
> the gate of heaven."
>
> — Entrance antiphon, Mass for the Blessed Virgin Mary, Gate of Heaven

Imagine for a moment that you are a young girl of perhaps sixteen years of age. You have been very protected by your family and so you know little of the world, but one thing you do know is that your life will have few surprises. You are betrothed to a good man and will soon marry. You will assume the duties of wife and then mother, just as have all the women of your family, all the women of the village in which you have always lived — all the women of the world, as far as you know. And then in one luminous moment that is both wonderful and terrible, you are confronted with a choice that is beyond all imagination. You may continue the life that you have always known ... or you can choose the impossible. You know that to choose the impossible is to risk everything. Your life will become unrecognizable; in fact, all things will be forever different. Reason tells you to cling to what you know, but something deeper than reason — some divine turmoil — swirls within you, and you utter a few words that will open the gates of heaven: "Let it be to me according to your word" (Lk 1:38).

This is the moment of the Annunciation, and it is a moment unlike any other, a moment that brought heaven and earth resoundingly together. Yet, it happened only because Mary of Nazareth chose what she could not begin to comprehend and trusted in God to do the impossible. From that moment on, she can rightly be called the Gate of Heaven, for through her God receives humanity and enters our frail lives; through her the rupture between God and His human creation begins to be healed; through her humanity becomes joined in an unbreakable embrace with divinity. Mary not only opens the gates of heaven, but she becomes the very gate through which light and graces will forever flow.

When I contemplate this title of our Blessed Mother, I am always overcome with a profound sense of awe and wonder. It reminds me clearly and even a little starkly of the immensity of her role in our salvation. The ultimate fate of everyone who has ever lived and everyone who ever will be depended on her, on her human will, on her love of God and her willingness to accept the unknown and incomprehensible with trust. What if she had recoiled and run away? What if she had made the safe choice? Where would we be?

This title of Our Lady also reminds me of the humility of God in a way that few things do. Think of the intensity of the love that is shown when God chooses to redeem mankind not by divine fiat but in a partnership with a young girl. In the Annunciation, God enters the world not with thunder and lightning and the giving of laws, but in the conception of a child who will grow slowly in the womb of this same young girl, who will depend on her for His life, who will be her obedient and loving son.

Our Blessed Mother has many titles, but the one we consider here is among the most significant, for it makes the others possible. Mary is forever our Gate of Heaven, for through her there came to shine on us Christ, the Light of the World.

Prayer

Loving Mother of the Redeemer, Gate of Heaven, Star of the Sea, assist your people who have fallen yet strive to rise again. To the wonderment of nature you bore your Creator, yet remained a virgin after, as before. You who received Gabriel's joyful greeting, have pity on us poor sinners. Amen.

48

Jesus, Zealous Lover of Souls

> "Jesus, lover of my soul, let me to Thy bosom fly,
> While the nearer waters roll, while the tempest still is high.
> Hide me, O my Savior, hide, till the storm of life is past;
> Safe into the haven guide; O receive my soul at last.
> Other refuge have I none, hangs my helpless soul on Thee;
> Leave, ah! Leave me not alone, still support and comfort me.
> All my trust on Thee is stayed, all my help from Thee I bring;
> Cover my defenseless head with the shadow of Thy wing."
>
> Charles Wesley, "Jesus, Lover of My Soul"

The above quotation consists of two stanzas from a hymn called "Jesus, Lover of My Soul," written by the eighteenth-century Protestant hymn writer Charles Wesley. I wish I could have included the entire hymn on this page, but it was simply too long. I urge you to read the rest of Wesley's beautiful work. It can be a great source of meditation on the overwhelming love of Christ for us. Here, we find a view of Jesus that seems very different from the one we encounter in titles such as Christ, the King of the Universe, or Christ, the King of Glory. Here, we see Christ's great love narrowed but not dimmed in any way. This hymn speaks to what may be called one of the deepest matters of the human heart, for it speaks of a God who burns with love and tenderness not just for His magnificent creation but for each part of it, for each individual — for you, for me. Here, Christ is shown as the zealous and tender lover, not simply of souls but of *my* soul. Wesley's hymn speaks of a deep reality, of the possibility of an intimate relationship with Jesus Christ that is so intense and personal that it overcomes all the problems, all the losses, all the tragedies, and all the disappointments of human life. It speaks of a relationship that can finally bring wholeness to our broken lives, a relationship that gives an answer — the only possible answer — to the great yearning in every human soul for a love that will not die.

All human lives desperately need this relationship simply in order to survive. Without it, we are cast adrift in a sea of mere things — things that will not last, that will one day disappear. In the hymn, the writer says of Christ: "Other refuge I have none, hangs my helpless soul on Thee." It is hard for me to think of truer words than these, and these words become truer for me with every passing year. I am reaching the end of my time on earth, and in my nearly eighty years I have come to understand, in a very personal way, that all things end, that all human power will one day be exhausted, that all that I know and love will decay and pass away. But Christ, who loves my soul with an unimaginable intensity, will not pass away. He will neither fade nor change. His love for me will never lessen. He remains constant; He remains "my rock and my redeemer" (Ps 19:14).

It is this knowledge, this assurance, to which the Christian clings. It is this understanding that gives us hope and even joy as we face the storms and tempests of life. We know that we never face them alone: Christ, the Zealous Lover of our Souls, is with us, bearing us up when we fall and healing us when we are injured. His love for each individual soul is inexhaustible, so inexhaustible that it keeps us alive even after our brief day on earth is done.

When next you look at a picture of the Sacred Heart, think of this: Know that the burning heart you see on the breast of Jesus burns with zealous love for your individual soul. Remember that this is a fire than can never be extinguished; it is a flame that will burn for all eternity. If you are ever tempted to forget His love, I urge you to meditate on His words at the Last Supper: "Father, I desire that they also, whom thou hast given me, may be with me where I am" (Jn 17:24). Know that He will pursue you in love, until you are with Him forever. Remember that the heart of Christ is forever ablaze for love of *you*!

Prayer

Blessed Lord and Lover of Souls, it was for our salvation that You became man and offered Your most precious Body and Blood on the Cross. Help us always to keep Your sacrifice in the forefront of our minds and Your love in the depths of our hearts, and never let us be parted from You. We ask this in Your most holy Name. Amen.

49
Our Lady of Guadalupe

"Our Lady went into a strange country
And they crowned her for a queen,
For she needed never to be stayed or questioned
But only seen;
And they were broken down under unbearable beauty
As we have been."

— G. K. Chesterton, "Going After the Lost Sheep"

If you have ever visited the Basilica of Our Lady of Guadalupe in the northeastern part of Mexico City, you will immediately know why the people of that land have been "broken down under unbearable beauty," as the above poem says. They are a people in love with the Virgin, and rightly so, because she chose them for God's special favor. The Virgin Mary, under the title of Our Lady of Guadalupe, appeared in Mexico five times in December 1531, just after the people of Mexico were liberated from the tyranny of a paganism so extreme that it involved human sacrifice. She won the people over with love, not force, and captured their hearts, imprinting upon them the love of Christ her son in a way that has rarely been seen in the history of the world.

Imprinting is perhaps the best word to describe Mary's effect on the people of that land, because she left behind an impression of herself on a poor Indian's cloak. The cloak is called a *tilma*, and you can see the original *tilma* — with the picture of Mary — hanging in the basilica even to this day. It is as pristine, pure and beautiful as the day it was given in 1531. Have you ever had an experience that struck you so profoundly that you say something like, "This will remain engraved upon my memory forever!" Well, that indeed was the effect of the apparitions of Mary on the Mexican people, who remain resolutely Catholic and perhaps even more resolutely lovers of the Virgin Mary. No one knows how the image got on the cloak or remains there. We must simply say it was a miracle of grace. It is not painted or dyed or brushed on the cloak in any way. Only God could have imprinted this image in the rough fibers of the cloak, and because it is a work of grace, the *tilma* communicates a vitality that continues to change hearts and souls as only Mary can.

It is impossible to describe all the miraculous aspects of the *tilma* in the short space I have here, but suffice it to say that when you look at that image, you see beauty itself. The *tilma* breathes the very aroma of a mother's love to the people who see it, and as surely as we know our own mothers, the people of that land, rich and poor, recognized a heavenly visitation of the Mother of Christ when they saw her image in their midst. It is evident in their faces and their bearing. They come to the Basilica of Our Lady of Guadalupe with every manner of prayer and petition to bring to God through Our Lady. In the apparition, she said that was her purpose for coming: "I want very much to have a little house built here for me, in which I ... will give [my son] to the people in all my personal love, in my compassion, in my help, in my protection. ... Here I will hear their weeping, their complaints, and heal all their sorrows, hardships, and sufferings."

Of all the sights I have seen at the basilica, I believe the most touching is the young Mexican mothers bringing their newborn children to Mary and holding them up in front of the *tilma* to "consecrate" them in a very humble but real way to their Mother who knows all the joys and sorrows of motherhood. You can also see the Mexicans literally walking on their knees from the large plaza into the basilica in fulfillment of oaths that they made to the Virgin in return for some favor. Words cannot describe how inspiring such a scene is to a Catholic from the United States. The sheer simplicity and strength of the faith in those souls reminds us that the Church is not a bureaucracy but rather a pilgrimage, and Our Lady walks with us through "this valley of tears."

Have you let Mary imprint her love upon your soul? Do you have a desperate need to bring to her? Would you approach her on your knees (symbolically at least), asking her help in some vital matter? She is waiting, in all her "unbearable beauty," to appear to you in some concrete way that will help you and make of you a true disciple. In the same way she made a whole nation come to Christ when they were in the grip of evil, of hopelessness, and despair.

Prayer

Blessed Mary, wonderful evangelizer of the Americas and lover of souls, open our hearts and minds to the love of Christ that comes to us through your merciful intercession, and lead us from the sins of this world to the promises of eternal life. We ask this through Jesus Christ, your Son, who is Lord and God forever and ever. Amen.

50

Heart of Christ, Burning Furnace of Charity

"*Ite, omnia incendite et inflammate!*
Go forth, set the whole world on fire,
and inflame all things!"

— Words of Saint Ignatius Loyola for Jesuits going to the foreign missions

In virtually every country I have visited in my many travels, I have noticed (usually in a nation's capital) the equivalent of the Tomb of the Unknown Soldier. Next to it is always some sort of eternal-flame monument commemorating the war dead of that country. Our version of this is in Arlington National Cemetery near Washington, D.C., at the tomb of President John F. Kennedy. But why is it that nations feel the need to memorialize their deceased loved ones with an eternal flame of some sort? In fact, of course, there is nothing eternal about these man-made flames at all, but there is something deeply relevant about the symbolism of a fire that is not quenched, that burns constantly out of love and remembrance. It is the intuition that we humans have deep in our hearts of an infinite love that cannot be extinguished, a love that glows ardently in the very center of all reality and has our salvation as its sole concern. That love is the love of the Heart of Christ. All our efforts at creating eternal flames are really just efforts to symbolize or reflect this burning divine love. The real purpose of our eternal flames is to remind ourselves of that eternal love.

The fascinating image of the burning bush in the Book of Exodus (see Chapter 3) is the biblical precedent to the loving Heart of Christ. We all remember the bush that "was aflame but not consumed" by the fire. The whole area around the bush was holy ground, and Moses had to take off his sandals to approach the Lord, who spoke from the Burning Bush. This was a fire so sacred that it made everything around it sacred. We remember also that in the dialogue between Moses and Yahweh, God revealed His Name and His desire to save His people from slavery in Egypt. In a sense, this passage is a tremendous expression of God's devotion to us. If we could look into the heart of the burning bush we would be awestruck by the saving love of God for His people. I am reminded here of the words of Jesus to Blessed Angela of Foligno, a thirteenth-century mystic whose visions of Jesus predate even those of the Sacred Heart to Saint Margaret Mary. Jesus said, "Look closely at my Heart. Is there anything there that is not love?" The Heart of Christ is the Burning Furnace of Charity for all souls throughout all of human history. We are the objects of His immense love!

I'm sure you have not have failed to notice the rather tepid spirituality of our times. I speak mostly of the institutionalized religious institutions and churches like our own beloved Catholic Church, which I sometimes think needs to have a fire lit underneath it to get our souls back into a truly devotional mode. We have clearly lost much of the profound reverence that was so common in my youth, a time when our Church was more devotional, a time when our prayers were more intense and seemed to spring from the deep parts of our souls. I am sure that God will bring that back in time, but it seems we respond almost coolly to the ever-burning love of God for us, and this is a shame.

Here's some news for you: This very moment — don't even bother to put this book down! — is the time to ask Jesus to pour into our hearts the immense richness of His eternal, burning love for all humanity. Let us repent of any sins we have committed against others since those people are the very souls that Christ loves with an infinite burning charity. Let us commit to the Burning Furnace of Charity all our intentions for the salvation of others, all our sins, sloth, and tepidity of soul, and ask Christ to inflame our hearts to be more like His own. We need have no fear of getting burned by getting closer to the Burning Furnace of Charity. Our only real fear should be not burning hot enough to inflame the whole world with Christ's Love.

Prayer

O burning, consuming, radiant Heart of Christ, font of all love and devotion for men, immerse our poor hearts in the depths of Your infinite charity, and help us to know all the love with which You have loved the world from the beginning of time. Give us grace to set the whole world on fire for love of You. We ask this in Your most holy Name. Amen.

Afterword

And so we have come to the end of our contemplation of a few of the titles of our Divine Savior and His Immaculate Mother. I hope that the reader has found this little journey as profitable as I have. I discovered in it an opportunity to deepen my relationship with Christ and with Our Lady. I was ablt to look again at things I had not thought of for awhile — sometimes for many years. The contemplation of some of these titles brought me back to my childhood; others returned me to the days when I was new and uncertain in the religious life. Each title has meant something important to me, and I hope to you as well.

The titles we have contemplated come from many sources and many time periods. Yet, each of them came into being as a result of a spiritual need, or perhaps a new way of perceiving a spiritual reality. I hope that you will continue to explore these titles of Jesus and Mary and the many more that the Church offers to us. The Litany of Loreto and the Litany of the Holy Name of Jesus are included at the back of this book to help you in this. Perhaps you might like to investigate the many images that are associated with these titles. Some of the paintings and icons upon which these titles are based are of great beauty. Many are themselves a real source of prayer and contemplation.

It is my hope and my prayer that your devotional life has been intensified in some way by this book. It is also my hope and prayer that you will never cease praising the glorious names of our Divine Savior and His Blessed Mother in this life, and that you will joyfully continue such praise for all eternity in the next.

Two Beautiful Litanies

Following are the two litanies from which I have drawn many of the titles about which I have written in this book. Both of these litanies are centuries old and are part of the Church's rich and beautiful patrimony of prayer. I hope they will become an important addition to the reader's prayer life.

The Litany of Loreto

Lord have mercy on us.
Lord have mercy on us.
Christ have mercy on us.
Christ have mercy on us.
Lord have mercy on us.
Lord have mercy on us.
Christ, hear us.
Christ, graciously hear us.
God the Father of Heaven, *have mercy on us.*
God the Son, Redeemer of the world, *have mercy on us.*
God the Holy Spirit, *have mercy on us.*
Holy Trinity, one God, *have mercy on us.*
Holy Mary, *pray for us.*
Holy Mother of God, *pray for us.*
Holy Virgin of virgins, *pray for us.*
Mother of Christ, *pray for us.*
Mother of divine grace, *pray for us.*
Mother most pure, *pray for us.*
Mother most chaste, *pray for us.*
Mother inviolate, *pray for us.*
Mother undefiled, *pray for us.*
Mother most amiable, *pray for us.*
Mother most admirable, *pray for us.*
Mother of good counsel, *pray for us.*
Mother of our Creator, *pray for us.*
Mother of our Redeemer, *pray for us.*
Virgin most prudent, *pray for us.*
Virgin most venerable, *pray for us.*

Virgin most renowned, *pray for us.*
Virgin most powerful, *pray for us.*
Virgin most merciful, *pray for us.*
Virgin most faithful, *pray for us.*
Mirror of justice, *pray for us.*
Seat of wisdom, *pray for us.*
Cause of our joy, *pray for us.*
Spiritual vessel, *pray for us.*
Vessel of honor, *pray for us.*
Singular vessel of devotion, *pray for us.*
Mystical rose, *pray for us.*
Tower of David, *pray for us.*
Tower of ivory, *pray for us.*
House of gold, *pray for us.*
Ark of the covenant, *pray for us.*
Gate of Heaven, *pray for us.*
Morning Star, *pray for us.*
Health of the sick, *pray for us.*
Refuge of sinners, *pray for us.*
Comforter of the afflicted, *pray for us.*
Help of Christians, *pray for us.*
Queen of Angels, *pray for us.*
Queen of Patriarchs, *pray for us.*
Queen of Prophets, *pray for us.*
Queen of Apostles, *pray for us.*
Queen of Martyrs, *pray for us.*
Queen of Confessors, *pray for us.*
Queen of Virgins, *pray for us.*
Queen of all Saints, *pray for us.*
Queen conceived without original sin, *pray for us.*
Queen of the most holy Rosary, *pray for us.*
Queen of families, *pray for us.*
Queen of peace, *pray for us.*
Lamb of God, Who takes away the sins of the world: *Spare us, O Lord.*
Lamb of God, Who takes away the sins of the world: *Graciously hear us, O Lord.*

Lamb of God, Who takes away the sins of the world: *Have mercy on us.*
Pray for us, most holy Mother of God,
That we may be made worthy of the promises of Christ.
Let us pray.

O God, whose only begotten Son, by his life, death and resurrection has purchased for us the rewards of eternal life, grant, we beseech you, that while meditating on the mysteries of the most holy rosary of the Blessed Virgin Mary, we may imitate what they contain and obtain what they promise, through Christ our Lord. Amen.

The Litany of the Most Holy Name of Jesus

Lord, have mercy.
Christ, have mercy.
Lord, have mercy.
Jesus, hear us.
Jesus, graciously hear us.
God, the Father of Heaven, *have mercy on us.*
God the Son, Redeemer of the world, *have mercy on us.*
God, the Holy Spirit, *have mercy on us.*
Holy Trinity, one God, *have mercy on us.*
Jesus, Son of the living God, *have mercy on us.*
Jesus, Splendor of the Father, *have mercy on us.*
Jesus, Brightness of eternal Light, *have mercy on us.*
Jesus, King of Glory, *have mercy on us.*
Jesus, Sun of Justice, *have mercy on us.*
Jesus, Son of the Virgin Mary, *have mercy on us.*
Jesus, most amiable, *have mercy on us.*
Jesus, most admirable, *have mercy on us.*
Jesus, the mighty God, *have mercy on us.*
Jesus, Father of the world to come, *have mercy on us.*
Jesus, angel of great counsel, *have mercy on us.*
Jesus, most powerful, *have mercy on us.*
Jesus, most patient, *have mercy on us.*
Jesus, most obedient, *have mercy on us.*

Jesus, meek and humble of heart, *have mercy on us.*
Jesus, Lover of Chastity, *have mercy on us.*
Jesus, our Lover, *have mercy on us.*
Jesus, God of Peace, *have mercy on us.*
Jesus, Author of Life, *have mercy on us.*
Jesus, Model of Virtues, *have mercy on us.*
Jesus, zealous for souls, *have mercy on us.*
Jesus, our God, *have mercy on us.*
Jesus, our Refuge, *have mercy on us.*
Jesus, Father of the Poor, *have mercy on us.*
Jesus, Treasure of the Faithful, *have mercy on us.*
Jesus, good Shepherd, *have mercy on us.*
Jesus, true Light, *have mercy on us.*
Jesus, eternal Wisdom, *have mercy on us.*
Jesus, infinite Goodness, *have mercy on us.*
Jesus, our Way and our Life, *have mercy on us.*
Jesus, joy of the Angels, *have mercy on us.*
Jesus, King of the Patriarchs, *have mercy on us.*
Jesus, Master of the Apostles, *have mercy on us.*
Jesus, Teacher of the Evangelists, *have mercy on us.*
Jesus, Strength of Martyrs, *have mercy on us.*
Jesus, Light of Confessors, *have mercy on us.*
Jesus, Purity of Virgins, *have mercy on us.*
Jesus, Crown of all Saints, *have mercy on us.*
Be merciful, *spare us, O Jesus.*
Be merciful, *graciously hear us, O Jesus.*
From all evil, *deliver us, O Jesus.*
From all sin, *deliver us, O Jesus.*
From your wrath, *deliver us, O Jesus.*
From the snares of the devil, *deliver us, O Jesus.*
From the spirit of fornication, *deliver us, O Jesus.*
From everlasting death, *deliver us, O Jesus.*
From the neglect of your inspirations, *deliver us, O Jesus.*
Through the mystery of your holy Incarnation, *deliver us, O Jesus.*
Through your Nativity, *deliver us, O Jesus.*
Through your Infancy, *deliver us, O Jesus.*
Through your most divine Life, *deliver us, O Jesus.*

Through your Labors, *deliver us, O Jesus.*
Through your Agony and Passion, *deliver us, O Jesus.*
Through your Cross and Dereliction, *deliver us, O Jesus.*
Through your Sufferings, *deliver us, O Jesus.*
Through your Death and Burial, *deliver us, O Jesus.*
Through your Resurrection, *deliver us, O Jesus.*
Through your Ascension, *deliver us, O Jesus.*
Through your Institution of the Most Holy Eucharist, *deliver us, O Jesus.*
Through your Joys, *deliver us, O Jesus.*
Through your Glory, *deliver us, O Jesus.*
Lamb of God, who take away the sins of the world, *spare us, O Jesus.*
Lamb of God, who take away the sins of the world, graciously *hear us, O Jesus.*
Lamb of God, who take away the sins of the world, *have mercy on us, O Jesus.*
Jesus, hear us.
Jesus, graciously hear us.
Let us pray.

O Lord Jesus Christ, you have said, "Ask and you shall receive; seek, and you shall find; knock, and it shall be opened to you"; mercifully attend to our supplications, and grant us the grace of your most divine love, that we may love you with all our hearts, and in all our words and actions, and never cease to praise you.

Make us, O Lord, to have a perpetual fear and love of your holy Name, for you never fail to govern those whom you solidly establish in your love. You, who live and reign forever and ever. Amen.